Battleground S

ISANDLWANA

Battleground South Africa
ISANDLWANA

Ian Knight
&
Ian Castle

Pen & Sword Books Limited
47 Church Street, Barnsley, South Yorkshire

For Vesna and Carolyn.
They have stood on these fields of conflict and come to
understand how much they mean to us.

First published in 2000 by
LEO COOPER
an imprint of
Pen & Sword Books Limited
47 Church Street, Barnsley, South Yorkshire S70 2AS

Copyright © Ian Knight & Ian Castle

ISBN 0 85052 656 6

A CIP catalogue record of this book is available
from the British Library

Printed by Redwood Books Limited
Trowbridge, Wiltshire

For up-to-date information on other titles produced under the Leo Cooper imprint,
please telephone or write to:

Pen & Sword Books Ltd, FREEPOST, 47 Church Street
Barnsley, South Yorkshire S70 2AS
Telephone 01226 734222

CONTENTS

Ngoza kaLudaba in full regalia, with young warriors. This photograph gives an excellent impression of Zulu 'full dress', although it does not show that of an *ibutho* of Cetshwayo's army, as this clan had split away. On campaign warriors would remove most of their furs and feathers.

Foreword

TRAVEL IN SOUTH AFRICA

The Anglo-Zulu War of 1879 remains one of the most intriguing British military campaigns of the 19th century. Indeed, its appeal today far outweighs its contemporary strategic and political significance, important though that was within the context of southern African history. This is largely because the war has come to be seen in Britain as the archetypal Imperial adventure, and the image of stalwart redcoats defending the far-flung corners of Empire has come to symbolize much of Britain's colonial experience. While such imagery has an undeniable appeal, there is, of course, another side of the story, for the war was essentially an act of Imperial aggression which brought misery to the Zulu kingdom, and helped pave the way for the difficulties experienced by South Africa's black population throughout the twentieth century.

In covering the battlefields of the war in two books, it was necessary to make an arbitrary divide. No doubt each visitor will want to make up his own itinerary, but in describing the battles we envisaged a tour approach to the sites in two broad arcs. The first, travelling from Durban via Pietermaritzburg, Greytown and Helpmekaar, considers the sites on the Natal side of the Mzinyathi (Buffalo) river, then travels north to look at the operations of the northern column. The towns of Dundee and Vryheid, an hour apart by road, would serve as a base for these. The second tour begins with Isandlwana, on the Zulu side of the Mzinyathi, then visits Ulundi, before returning to Durban via the sites of the British coastal column. Of course, with both books, the discerning traveller can mix and match at will.

As this is the second book in the series, we have given only cursory treatment to the causes of the war, which were covered in detail in the *Rorke's Drift* BATTLEGROUND title. For ease of reading, we have nonetheless described the war – in so far as it is possible – in chronological order; you may need to dip in and out of the text, according to your itinerary!

It has never been easier to visit the battlefields of Zululand than today. Nevertheless, independent travellers are advised to take a few basic precautions. Public transport is virtually non-existent, so those planning to travel on their own, rather than with a tour, will need to hire a car. Many of the sites remain remote and require long journeys down dirt roads to reach them; be prepared for this, and don't attempt it in bad weather, when heavy rain can still turn a road surface into unforgiving grease in a remarkably short time. Always allow plenty of time for every journey and do not travel by night; to be lost in rural Zululand in the dark can be an unnerving experience. Always fill up with petrol before a journey, since petrol stations in rural areas can be few and far between, and it's worth noting that in South Africa you cannot pay for petrol with standard credit cards. While sites such as Rorke's Drift and Isandlwana are not physically demanding to the visitor, others such as Hlobane, should not be attempted without local advice. The rugged nature of the terrain, and its sheer remoteness, can present risks to the unwary. And yes, there are snakes out there, so strong walking boots and a handy stick are essential for any hike.

There has been a steady increase in the availability of tourist accommodation in the last ten years, particularly in the principal battlefield areas. A number of luxury lodges have been opened on farms surrounding Isandlwana and Rorke's Drift, indeed, a new lodge has just opened overlooking Isandlwana itself, and while these offer good food, tranquil settings and plenty of entertaining stories, they are not cheap, even allowing for the exchange rate. Other areas of the war are not yet so well served, although Ulundi offers a choice of a Holiday Inn or, as part of the oNdini museum complex, a traditional-style Zulu homestead. In the Eshowe region there are a number of good establishments offering a Zulu cultural experience which are within easy driving distance of the historic sites. At the cheaper end of the market, however, the traveller is best accompanied by a good sense of humour, as ideas of service in Africa can differ markedly from those in Europe or the US.

It must also be admitted that crime can be a problem in South Africa, and the traveller is best advised to display the same common sense he would inevitably show in any country with a large population living below the poverty line. Do not walk the streets draped with conspicuous valuables, do not visit townships without a local guide and ask local advice if you are unsure about the safety of an area you wish to visit.

Finally, for those who have been drawn to the battlefields by a passion for the 1964 feature-film *Zulu*, it is worth noting that this was not filmed at the battlefield of Rorke's Drift, but rather at the Royal Natal Park, in the Drakensberg (Kahlamba) mountains. Should you wish to visit this area, a variety of accommodation is available in the Park, though sadly nothing remains beyond the distinctive landscape to indicate exactly where the film was shot. Much of the 1979 movie *Zulu Dawn* – about Isandlwana – was, however, filmed at Siphezi mountain, mid-way along the Nquthu-Babanango road, and not far from Isandlwana itself.

Durnford's men join the Natal Volunteers lining the donga at Isandlwana, as portrayed in the 1979 film *Zulu Dawn*.the mountain in the background is Siphezi, which doubled for Isandlwana during filming.

Ntombe

Luneburg

Phongolo

Utrecht

Khambula

Mkhuze

Hlobane

N

Mzinyathi (Buffalo)

Ncome (Blood)

wcastle

Dundee

Prince
Imperial

Black

Rorke's
Drift

Ulundi

Mfolozi

Isandlwana

White

Helpmekaar

Mhlatuze

Eshowe

Nyezane

Greytown

Thukela

Gingindlovu

INDIAN
OCEAN

Fort
Pearson

BATTLEFIELDS AND
HISTORICAL SITES FEATURED IN

BATTLEGROUND
SOUTH AFRICA

Pietermaritzburg

"RORKE'S DRIFT" &
"ISANDLWANA"

Durban

25   50   75   100

Kilometres

9

King Cetshwayo kaMpande, ruler of the Zulu nation. His kingdom stood in the way of British expansion in South Africa – he would have to be provoked into fight with the British Empire.

Chapter One

THE ROAD TO WAR

The Zulu kingdom emerged in the region of present-day KwaZulu/Natal under the famous King Shaka, in the 1820s. In Shaka's time, it stretched from the Zulu heartland – along the banks of the White Mfolozi river – northwards beyond the Black Mfolozi and southwards across the Thukela river, into Natal proper. Not until towards the end of its independent existence, when it was hemmed in by colonial neighbours, were the kingdom's borders static; they ebbed and flowed, according to the support of the various African groups on the periphery. The first whites arrived to establish a settlement at Port Natal – now Durban – in 1824 and they thrived under King Shaka's protection. Even by the 1830s, however, the growth in white influence had become so marked that the Zulu abandoned claims to the loyalty of many African chiefdoms lying south of the Thukela and in 1843 Natal became a British colony.

The underlying causes of conflict in 1879 were the growth in white economic activity, land hunger and changing views of the British imperial mission in Africa. For fifty years Natal and the Zulu kingdom co-existed peacefully, despite occasional political crises; then, in the 1870s, the British adopted a new forward policy, stimulated by the prospect of a nascent regional economy, a vision fuelled by newly discovered mineral wealth. In simplistic terms, the British wished to extend their influence and the Zulu kingdom was in the way. The problem became acute following the British annexation of the Boer republic of the Transvaal in 1877, since the Transvaal had a long-standing border dispute with the Zulu, which the British now inherited. At the end of 1878, the local British representative – Sir Henry Bartle Frere, the High Commissioner for Southern Africa – provoked a quarrel with the Zulu kingdom.

On 11 January 1879, the Anglo-Zulu War began.

The senior British commander in southern Africa, Lieutenant General Lord Chelmsford, was constrained by Frere's political aims to undertake an offensive strategy. With his experience of colonial warfare shaped by his recent experience on the Eastern Cape (9th Cape Frontier War, 1877-78), Chelmsford was confident that his superior firepower would ensure him victory in open battle. His priority, therefore, was to drive the Zulu into a corner and make them fight. He

GRAPH BY ELLIOT & FRY

Lieutenant General Lord Chelmsford; the senior British commander in southern Africa.

was also convinced that the Zulu would avoid a confrontation, for the same reason. These preconceptions entirely shaped his strategic planning and in the event circumstances would prove the assumptions upon which they were based to be sadly mistaken.

Chelmsford had initially hoped to invade Zululand in five separate columns, from roughly equi-distant points along the Natal and Transvaal borders, which would then converge on King Cetshwayo kaMpande's principal homestead, oNdini (known to the British by a variant of the same word, Ulundi). In the event, however, he had too few troops and logistical facilities for such a comprehensive plan, while the fact that Frere did not enjoy the full support of the home government meant that he was unlikely to be reinforced. As a result he was forced to reduce his five offensive columns to three, while the remaining two were reduced in size and given largely supporting roles.

In late 1878, as political events moved inexorably towards a confrontation, Chelmsford assembled his columns on the Zulu borders. The offensive columns were placed at the Lower Thukela Drift, in eastern Natal, near the coast; at Rorke's Drift on the Mzinyathi, along the central border and at Utrecht in the Transvaal, to the north. They were designated nos. 1, 3 and 4 respectively and were commanded by Colonel Charles Pearson, Colonel Richard Glyn, and Colonel H. Evelyn Wood. Chelmsford himself decided to accompany the Centre Column – a decision which effectively deprived Colonel Glyn of much

Men of the 24th Regiment, who formed the backbone of the Centre Column.

of his authority. The defensive columns, Nos. 2 and 5, were situated at the Middle Drift on the Thukela, between the Lower and Rorke's Drifts and at the hamlet of Derby, in the Transvaal. They were commanded by Brevet Colonel Anthony Durnford and Colonel Hugh Rowlands VC.

The Zulu king, Cetshwayo kaMpande, watched the British build up with foreboding. Since he had not sought a confrontation, he decided to adopt a defensive strategy, to fight the British only where they had invaded Zulu soil. In early January he assembled his army at oNdini, in order to prepare them ritually for war. Although his council discussed a number of possible responses, they deliberately left the initiative to the British, not wanting to be seen as the agressor, waiting to see which of Chelmsford's columns would prove the most threatening. Although the Zulu army was undoubtedly outclassed in terms of firepower, such was their spirit that, ironically, they too sought to resolve the war by a decisive clash in the open.

Chelmsford's Centre Column assembled on the Biggarsberg ridge, high above the Mzinyathi (Buffalo) valley, in November 1878. Chelmsford had chosen the tiny hamlet of Helpmekaar – no more than a church and a few sheds – as the rendezvous, not only because of its strategic location, but because the prevailing breeze was believed to keep it free of horse sickness.

The backbone of Chelmsford's column were the two battalions of the 24th Regiment (2nd Warwickshires). The battalion – rather than the regiment – was the principal British infantry tactical unit in the 1870s and where a regiment had more than one battalion, in theory it was unlikely that the two would serve together in action. This was because one battalion was always supposed to be on garrison duty in the UK, while the other was posted overseas. In fact, the demands of a rapidly expanding empire meant that more battalions were posted overseas at any given time than this system allowed. The 1/24th had been in South Africa since 1875 and had earned a good reputation as a steady and experienced battalion, which was acclimatized, had seen a good deal of action, and worked well under its officers. The 2/24th had only arrived in South Africa in 1878, in time to take part in the mopping up operations on the Cape Frontier. Fresh out from home, the men of the 2nd Battalion were markedly younger and less experienced than their 1st Battalion counterparts, but already showed every sign of adapting to life on active service in Africa. It is a myth that the 24th was composed entirely of Welshmen; while it is true that the regimental depot had been established in Brecon, in the Welsh borders, in 1873 – a move which had resulted in an increase in Welsh recruits – the regiment continued to draw its personnel from recruiting depots right across Great Britain. Like all Victorian units, it was composed of Englishmen, Welsh, Scots and Irishmen. The most that can be said is that the Welsh connection had resulted in a slightly higher proportion of Welshmen in the ranks compared to the national average.

For his artillery support, Chelmsford had just one battery of 7 pdr Rifled Muzzle-Loading (RML) guns – N Battery, 5th Brigade – under the command of a Colonel Arthur Harness. Harness' battery were also veterans of the Cape Frontier, where they had often worked alongside the 24th. The guns themselves were essentially light mountain guns, but had been mounted on heavier 9 pdr carriages, which were more suited to the rugged South African terrain. Throughout the war, the performance of the 7 pdr would be disappointing, because of its low muzzle velocity and small bursting charge.

Chelmsford began the war with no regular cavalry regiments and to make good the deficiency he had to rely heavily on local resources. During the Cape Frontier war, two squadrons of Mounted Infantry had been raised by the simple expedient of extracting volunteers from the Line battalions who could ride. Chelmsford had one squadron present with the column, but it was not enough. Instead, he had leaned heavily on the civilian authorities in Natal to authorize the deployment of the Natal Volunteer Corps in Zululand. The Volunteers were part-time soldiers, drawn from white settler society, and armed by the colonial government, but uniformed at their own expense. Officially raised for

A Levy Leader and some of his men. Chelmsford's operations would not have been possible without the support of thousands of African auxiliaries.

The camp at Helpmekaar. This photograph was taken later in the war, when the position had been fortified by the addition of earthwork ramparts.

defence only, Chelmsford was dependent on both the government's approval, and the agreement of individual Volunteers, if he wanted to use them on offensive operations outside the colony. In the event, most agreed, and Chelmsford had a handful of tiny mounted units attached to the Centre Column; the Buffalo Border Guard (twenty-five men), Newcastle Mounted Rifles (thirty-six men) and Natal Carbineers (sixty-one men). He also commanded the services of the quasi-military, full-time men of the Natal Mounted Police (150 men). Nevertheless, his total mounted element amounted to scarcely more than 300 men; too few, as events would prove, to provide an effective scouting screen for a column of this size.

To further increase his numbers, Chelmsford had also persuaded the colonial authorities to raise an auxiliary unit, made up from Natal's African population. This was a potentially rich source of recruitment, since many of the Natal chiefdoms had a history of animosity towards the Zulu kingdom. The Natal government was wary of this scheme, however, and it was nervous of arming its own black population for fear of insurrection. In the end, a compromise was reached which would please no one. Chelmsford was authorized to raise an auxiliary unit known as the Natal Native Contingent. Only one in ten of the recruits were given firearms, however, usually of obsolete patterns; the

The same view today. All that remains of the earthwork are faint depressions in the grass, foreground. The military cemetery lies to the immediate right of the trees.

rest had to provide their own traditional weapons. Early plans to issue them with outdated British uniforms were abandoned because of the cost, and instead the men were issued with a red rag, to be worn around the head or arm – the only obvious point of distinction from their Zulu enemies. The NNC was not raised until November 1878, on the very eve of hostilities, and had little opportunity to train. Indeed, it was generally at the bottom of the British list of priorities, and received scant resources or consideration. While a number of the white senior officers were appointed for their experience and reliability, the junior officers and white NCOs were made up from volunteers who were not wanted elsewhere. Many were adventurers from the irregular units of the Cape frontier, hard-bitten, ill-disciplined men who spoke little Zulu, and had nothing but contempt for the men under their command.

The Centre Column included the 3rd Regiment, NNC – two battalions strong, each of a thousand men. Among them were a number of political refugees from the Zulu kingdom, led by Prince Sikhota kaMpande, one of King Cetshwayo's own brothers, who had fled to Natal to avoid the fraternal blood-letting which had accompanied the king's succession. The regiment also included a large number of amaChunu people, whose chief, Pakhade, had a long history of dispute with the Zulu kings. Much might have been made of such material, under other circumstances.

In the first week of January 1879 Chelmsford's column moved down from the Helpmekaar heights and established a new camp on the bank of the Mzinyathi river, at Rorke's Drift. In all, the column consisted of 4,709 men, 302 wagons and carts, and over 1,500 transport oxen. Chelmsford knew that Cetshwayo's army had a theoretical strength in excess of 40,000 warriors and that the king could field up to 25,000 men at any given time. When, on 11th January, the war began, Chelmsford had little idea of the Zulu plans or movements, beyond the fact that Natal Border Agents had reported that Zulu living along the border had been called up to oNdini.

The column crossed into Zululand at dawn on the 11th. It was a cold, misty morning, and the 2/24th and artillery were posted on a rise overlooking the drift, to cover the crossing. While the mounted men crossed downstream, at Jim Rorke's old drift, the 1/24th were ferried across, a company at a time, in ponts – flat-bottomed ferries – which had been stretched across a deep pool upstream. The NNC were left to wade through water up to their armpits. There was a tense half-hour as the first troops reached the Zulu bank and spread out into the enveloping mist; then, suddenly, the mist lifted and the sun came out.

The Mzinyathi (Buffalo River) at Rorke's Drift. Shiyane hill dominates the skyline. It was here that Lord Chelmsford first crossed from Natal into Zululand in January 1879.

The only Zulu was a solitary herdsman who watched in astonishment from a nearby rise. The Anglo-Zulu War had begun in fine style.

The assembly point of the Centre Column, Helpmekaar, lies on the R33 Greytown/Dundee road. A hamlet in 1879, it is scarcely bigger today and consists largely of a police station and magistrates' court. The site of the original British camp – the only tangible remnant of which is the cemetery, where lie the remains of men who later died there of disease – is situated behind the police station. To reach it, it is necessary to go through a farm gate to the right of the ruined store, then walk behind the store, climbing through a couple of dilapidated fences.

From Helpmekaar a road branches off towards the Mzinyathi, signposted 'Rorke's Drift'. This is roughly the route taken by the column; much of the road is dirt track and should be approached with caution in wet weather. At the bottom of the escarpment both Shiyane hill, above the Rorke's Drift mission and Isandlwana are clearly visible. Shortly before Rorke's Drift, the road branches off again to the left, signposted 'Isandlwana'. A low bridge now crosses the river at roughly the point where Chelmsford invaded Zululand. Rorke's original drift was below the islands, downstream to the right; the rise

19

*to the left was where the guns and 2/24th were posted. The remains of
Fort Melvill – built later in the war to secure the crossing – can still be
seen on top of this rise. It was in the pool immediately to the left of the
bridge that the ponts operated. From the river, the road winds through
the Batshe valley towards Isandlwana Chelmsford's route was rather
more direct – off-country to the right – but the current road is close
enough to give the modern visitor a good sense of the column's
movements. Approaching a line of hills ahead there is a T-junction – go
right to Isandlwana. It was in the cliffs immediately to the left at this
point that the first action of the war – the skirmish with Sihayo's
followers – took place.*

Once on Zulu soil, Chelmsford established a sprawling new camp.
Ahead of him the road passed through the territory of Chief Sihayo
kaXongo, a local *induna* of considerable importance and a member of
the royal council. Chief Sihayo's sons had been involved in a border
violation which had been cited in the British ultimatum and for all
these reasons he seemed an ideal choice for Chelmsford's first act of
aggression. At dawn on the 12th four companies of the 1/24th, both
battalions of the NNC and the mounted contingent set out to attack
Sihayo. The expedition was nominally under the command of Colonel
Glyn but, typically, was accompanied by Chelmsford himself. Several
companies of the 2/24th were to start out later, to sweep through the
Batshe valley.

Chelmsford's party reached the Batshe – a shallow stream just a few
feet wide – without incident; but as they crossed the British were
challenged by Zulu hiding among boulders at the foot of a line of cliffs,
directly opposite. In fact, neither Chief Sihayo nor his senior son
Mehlokazulu was present in the valley, having attended the general
muster at oNdini. Sihayo had left another son, Mkhumbikazulu, and a
number of his retainers to guard his homes and crops. The Zulu had
taken up a position at the base of a horseshoe-shaped gorge, and dared
the British to attack them. And so Glyn did, sending his cavalry to the
right, to ascend the ridge above the cliffs further down, and ordering
the 24th to clamber up the slopes on the left. The bulk of the fighting
fell to the reluctant NNC, who were required to advance into the mouth
of the horseshoe. A fierce scrimmage broke out at close-quarters
among the boulders until the Zulu, realizing they were surrounded,
scrambled out of the boulders and back over the hills. About thirty of
them were left dead on the field, among them Mkhumbikazulu. Glyn's
successful command then spread out over the hills, rounding up cattle

The first action of the war; the skirmish at 'Sihayo's Stronghold' on 12th January 1879.

The Batshe river valley. Beyond the sandy riverbed is the horseshoe gorge on the western face of Ngedla mountain that was defended by Sihayo kaXongo's adherents on 12th January.

The route taken by the Centre Column towards Isandlwana, the top of which can be seen on the horizon. It is possible that the ruts to the left of the photo are part of the scarring, still visible today, left by the army wagons as they advanced over the wet ground.

and goats, and jeering at the 2/24th, who arrived too late to share in the action, beyond burning Sihayo's deserted homestead. British casualties amounted to three NNC killed and 18 wounded. That afternoon the expedition returned to the camp at Rorke's Drift in good spirits, despite a sudden thunderstorm which drenched them.

Chelmsford professed himself well pleased with the result. The Zulu had fought well – better than he had expected – but were no match for his men. A relaxed air of self-confidence pervaded the column.

Indeed, at this point in the campaign it seemed that the weather might prove Chelmsford's greatest obstacle to the invasion of Zululand. After years of drought, the summer rains had come with a vengeance, making life under canvas uncomfortable and turning the already inadequate tracks into a quagmire. It took over a week for his men to prepare the road ahead and it was not until the 20th that Chelmsford felt able to advance, moving the column forward to a distinctive rocky outcrop known to the Zulu as Isandlwana.

Once it became clear that the British were in earnest, King Cetshwayo mustered his army at the cluster of royal homesteads near oNdini, which constituted his capital, in the third week of January.

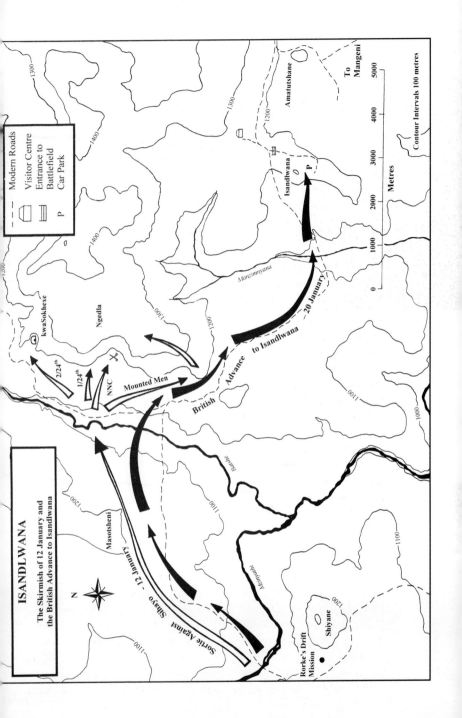

ISANDLWANA

The Skirmish of 12 January and
the British Advance to Isandlwana

N

Modern Roads
Visitor Centre
Entrance to
Battlefield
P   Car Park

Masotsheni

Sortie Against Sihayo — 12 January

Mounted Men
NNC
1/24th
2/24th

Ngedla

kwaSokhexe

British Advance to Isandlwana — 20 January

ManZimnyana

Isandlwana

P

Amatutshane

To
Mangeni

Batshe

Nxibongo

Shiyane

Rorke's Drift
Mission

Contour Intervals 100 metres

Metres

23

Pressed on three fronts, his council was reluctant to decide a strategy until news reached it of the attack on Sihayo's followers. Ironically, far from intimidating the Zulu, the skirmish merely served to mark out in Zulu eyes which of the columns was the most dangerous, and the king and his council shaped their response accordingly.

To mask the main response from the flanking columns, Zulu living in the northern and coastal districts were ordered to try to slow down the advance of the columns in their area. A small detachment of troops from oNdini was ordered to reinforce the coastal contingents, while the main army was sent across country directly, to attack the Centre Column. After days of ritual preparation – designed to encourage morale and achieve supernatural ascendancy over the enemy – the main army left oNdini on the 17th. It was commanded by two of the king's most trusted military advisers, Ntshingwayo kaMahole and Mavumengwana kaNdlela, and consisted of twelve full regiments, mostly young, unmarried warriors – the cream of the nation's manhood. Along the way it was joined by small contingents of men who, like Sihayo's followers, had been left at home to protect crops and livestock. By the time it neared Isandlwana, it numbered more than 25,000 men.

The first clear view of Isandlwana as seen by the soldiers of the Centre Column as they advanced on 20th January. To the right of the mountain the nek connects to Mahlabamkhosi (later known to the British as Black's Kop).

Chapter Two

ISANDLWANA – THE WARRIORS' BATTLE

Chelmsford established his camp on the forward slope of the foot of Isandlwana hill. The choice of site was dictated by the proximity of water and firewood, but in any case the camp commanded an impressive view along the further line of advance into Zululand. This view was closed in by a range of hills some twelve miles off to the front; by a high point and ridge known as Malakatha and Hlazakazi, several miles off to the right, and by a lower ridge – the iNyoni – much closer to the left. While his men began to unpack the wagons and set up blocks of tents at Isandlwana, Chelmsford himself rode out with his staff to scout the country ahead.

By this stage, the first rumour of a Zulu counter-attack had reached Chelmsford. With his recent experience on the Cape Frontier in mind he was concerned that, rather than attack him in the open, the Zulu would try to outflank him, and strike into Natal behind him. He was not unduly concerned about his left flank – the iNyoni heights were open enough, and Colonel Wood's Left Flank Column was in any case operating only forty miles away – but he was concerned with the Malakatha range. He rode out as far as the Mangeni gorge, at the far end of Hlazakazi, and examined the country beyond with field glasses. There, on his right flank, the country became rugged and broken, scoured by several small rivers which flowed down through a maze of jagged ridges to join the Mzinyathi. If a Zulu army got into such country, he feared, he would never get them out.

When he returned to Isandlwana that evening, he made plans for the Malakatha and Hlazakazi heights to be thoroughly scouted. At dawn on the 21st, the NNC was to march south, into the hills, then sweep eastwards. The mounted contingent was to scout the top of the range and the two groups were to meet up at the Mangeni gorge beyond. The whole force was commanded by Major John Dartnell, the experienced senior officer of the Mounted Police, and it was to return to camp by nightfall.

The reconnaissance set out as planned. The going was difficult, especially for the NNC, who had miles of rough and broken country to cover. Neither party encountered more than a handful of Zulu non-combatants before they met up near the head of the Mangeni that afternoon. Some of Dartnell's scouts, however, had spotted small

The camp at Isandlwana as depicted in a contemporary engraving.

parties of Zulu watching from the hills above the gorge and, rather than return to camp with nothing substantial to report, Dartnell decided to investigate. The NNC retired to the security of the Hlazakazi heights, while Dartnell's men rode tentatively into the hills opposite. They had not gone far when, according to Trooper Symons of the Carbineers:

'We anxiously watched the small party disappear over the brow of the hill and when we saw them riding down the rocky hill side at a much more rapid pace than when they went up we knew something was after them, and our surmise was correct for, from one end of the ridge to the other, as if by magic, rose a long line of black warriors advancing at the double in short intervals of skirmishing order. It was a magnificent spectacle, and no British regiments could excel in keeping their distances in skirmishing at the double. They uttered no sound and on reaching the brow of the hill their centre halted while their flanks came on thus forming the noted "horns" of the Zulu impis.

'We all thought we were to be attacked but a shout came from the hill top answered by one from the right horn. The impi then halted, another shout, and the Zulu slowly retired till only three or four [were] visible on the ridge...'

To the Volunteers, it seemed that the Zulu were trying to draw them into a trap, and Dartnell lost no time in withdrawing his men. Yet he was now in a dilemma; he had encountered Zulu more or less where Chelmsford had anticipated, but it was the close of the day, and he had no clear idea of the Zulu strength or intentions. Moreover, to return to Isandlwana now would leave a Zulu force in his rear in the dark. Dartnell decided to join the NNC on the heights, to remain overnight, and to send a message to Chelmsford immediately.

The road from Rorke's Drift to Isandlwana passes behind the mountain, giving the same spectacular view that Chelmsford's column would have enjoyed on the march. While the old wagon road passed below the southern pinnacle of the crag to the right, the present road runs further north, to the left of the mountain. It then continues eastwards, beyond Isandlwana, along the base of the iNyoni heights. To visit the camp site now you will need a ticket, obtainable from the Visitors' Centre at the foot of the iNyoni range, on your left. This Centre is built into part of the St. Vincent's Mission, which was established on the battlefield in 1880. From there one can return to the road and either go right, to enter the battlefield reserve, or left, to visit the site of Dartnell's encounter. In this direction, the road forks off to the right as it passes the distinctive 'Conical Koppie'; this is the way to Mangeni. There are some Zulu buildings on the left and a road cuts between them, heading out across the plain. The Malakatha and Hlazakazi ridge now close in on your right – this was the area scouted on the 21st. The road winds towards a further line of hills across your front, marked by another distinctive conical hill. Just before you reach it, look to your left – it was in here somewhere that Dartnell's encounter took place – while to your right, up onto the eastern end of Hlazakazi, is where his force bivouacked. The road then passes over a nek [a saddle between two hills] below the conical hill and descends into a basin, with a circle of hills on your left and the Mangeni gorge on your right. Somewhere in this basin Chelmsford had intended to make his next camp; he spent most of the 22nd skirmishing in the hills on your left. Look down the Mangeni, and see the wild country beyond, which caused him such concern.

When you return to Isandlwana, pause on the nek to look back at the mountain. It was from this area that Chelmsford's officers tried to discern events at the camp as the battle unfolded.

Dartnell's report reached Isandlwana just before 2 am on the 22nd January. Chelmsford did not hesitate much; here were the Zulu doing exactly what he expected. He gave orders for the 2/24th and four of Harness' guns to be made ready, as silently as possible, to march out to Mangeni. He intended to surprise the Zulu with a night march and attack them at dawn.

In fact, by the time he reached the Mangeni just after first light, the Zulu spotted by Dartnell had dispersed, apparently retiring away from the British into the hills to the north-east. Chelmsford was used to such incidents on the Cape Frontier; wearily, he ordered his men to sweep through the hills and desultory skirmishing lasted throughout the morning. There was no sign, however, of the main Zulu army.

As an afterthought, before leaving camp that morning, Chelmsford had instructed that a message be sent to Colonel Durnford, ordering him to move to Isandlwana.

Durnford is an intriguing and controversial character, whose actions had considerable impact on the events of the 22nd. A Royal Engineer, he had spent much of the previous decade in South Africa and had been wounded in 1873 during a botched operation to suppress a rather dismal 'rebellion' by one of Natal's African chiefdom's, the Hlubi of Chief Langalibalele. That incident had left him with a withered left arm – he wore it Napoleon style, thrust into the front of his jacket – and

28

The Mangeni gorge. Beyond the gorge there is a glimpse of the rugged ground to the south of Isandlwana which caused Lord Chelmsford concern. After the reconnaissance patrol of 21st January, Dartnell bivouacked on the high ground to the right of the photo.

Mangeni. This was the area which Lord Chelmsford selected on the morning of the 22nd as the next camp area for the Centre Column on the advance to Ulundi. Zulu movements in this area on 21st January had led Chelmsford to march from Isandlwana with half his force.

a sense that his reputation had been unjustly tarnished. He entered the Zulu War with something to prove. His standing as an outsider among the conservative military establishment was further enhanced by the fact that he liked and admired the African population, and indeed most of his command was black.

Durnford's column – No. 2 in the original scheme of things – had originally been posted on the escarpment above the Middle Drift of the Thukela. Here Durnford had shown rather too much independent initiative for Chelmsford's liking, and on the 14th Durnford had been ordered to march with part of his command to support Chelmsford at Rorke's Drift. He had arrived there just after Chelmsford had advanced to Isandlwana.

Although Chelmsford later claimed that on the 22nd he had intended Durnford to advance to Isandlwana and take command of the camp, his orders were later found on the battlefield and this was not the case. In fact Chelmsford, convinced that *he* was the one about to fight a battle, seems to have given no very clear thought to Durnford, beyond the fact that he wanted him closer at hand. Indeed, Chelmsford does not seem to have given much thought to the camp at all, and for the same reason.

Durnford arrived at Isandlwana at about 10.30 am, at the head of five troops of black cavalry – all armed with carbines and undoubtedly the best of the black auxiliary units – two infantry companies of the 1/1st NNC, and a rocket battery consisting of two 9 pdr rockets on troughs, under the command of Major F. Russell, RA.

He found that events at Isandlwana had moved on since the General had left before dawn.

Chelmsford had left five companies of the 1/24th at Isandlwana and one of the 2/24th, together with a detachment of his mounted men and a two-gun section of N/5 Battery.

Lieutenant-Colonel Henry Pulleine, 1/24th, whom Lord Chelmsford left in command of the camp at Isandlwana on 22nd January.

There were also at least two companies of the 3rd NNC in the camp and small detachments of Engineers, Hospital and Service Corps. This should have been enough to defend the camp, but his choice of commander in any case reflected the view that the site was not in danger. The senior officer was Colonel Henry Pulleine, an experienced officer with a flair for administration and organization, who had nonetheless never held a command in action before. Chelmsford's orders had been simple; Pulleine was to defend the camp.

When Durnford arrived, he was surprised to see that the 24th were formed up in front of their tents. There were no Zulu in sight but Pulleine explained that shortly after dawn a large body of the enemy had appeared on the iNyoni ridge, to the north of the camp. They made no attempt to attack, but watched the camp intently before retiring. Pulleine had prudently placed pickets on the edge of the heights and had stood the men to in readiness. Now that Durnford's men had arrived, the total British force consisted of just over 1,760 men, of whom roughly 700 were redcoats of the 24th, and nearly 800 were black.

This news intrigued Durnford. If he had expected to find fresh orders from Chelmsford, however, he was to be disappointed. Nor could Pulleine enlighten him as to the General's intentions in this regard. The situation was awkward, because Durnford was nominally senior to Pulleine, but was in fact the commander of a separate, independent column. Any ambiguity, however, played into Durnford's hands. He rightly realized that the situation had changed since Chelmsford's departure and he was concerned that Zulu movements on the iNyoni heights might be part of a Zulu attempt to cut Chelmsford off from the camp. He decided, therefore, not to remain in camp, but to sweep through the iNyoni hills, with a view to securing Chelmsford's left flank. He asked Pulleine to lend him some infantry, but Pulleine, remembering his commitment to defend the camp, demurred, and Durnford rode out with the breezy admonition that he would nonetheless expect to be supported if he got into difficulties.

Durnford left at about 11.30 am. He divided his force in two, sending two troops [i.e. of fifty men each] of the mounted auxiliaries up onto the ridge via a spur immediately to the north of Isandlwana. Their instructions were to drive any Zulu along the top of the heights, away from the camp. Durnford himself, with the rest of his command, rode straight out from the camp across the open plain, only following the curve of the hills to the north as they were lost to sight from Isandlwana.

The two troops on top of the heights, commanded by Lieutenants Raw and Roberts, and accompanied by Captain George Shepstone, had ridden several miles from the camp when they spotted a herd of cattle being driven frantically in the opposite direction by Zulu scouts. They gave chase, until about five miles from the camp the Zulu crested a boulder-strewn rise and disappeared beyond. As they rode after them, Raw's and Roberts' men suddenly had to reign in short.

Ahead of them, the ground dropped away sharply into a wide, open valley. Sitting quietly at the bottom of the valley were the 25,000 men of the main Zulu army.

The Zulu army had left oNdini on the 17th, travelling slowly so as not to tire the men. By the 20th it had reached Siphezi mountain, fifteen miles from Isandlwana as the crow flies. Then, on the 21st, while Chelmsford was looking for it south-west of Siphezi, it had moved north-west, into the Ngwebeni valley.

This was, perhaps, the one point in the entire campaign when it was acutely vulnerable to discovery. It was, in effect, passing across the front of the British army and in terrain which was more than usually open. Indeed, it was while this movement was taking place that a patrol from the camp nearly blundered into it; they were intercepted by Zulu scouts under Zibhebhu kaMaphitha, who were screening the advance, and driven off before they saw anything. The army moved in small

A view of the Ngwebeni valley from Mabaso. When Lieutenant Raw's troop of Zikhali's Horse arrived at this point, a little before noon on 22nd January, the valley below was filled with 25,000 warriors of the Zulu army.

Zibhebhu kaMaphitha, chief of the Mandlakazi section of the Royal House. Zibhebhu was one of the most able Zulu generals of his age; he commanded the Zulu scouts during the Isandlwana campaign.

groups, scattering across country, following the folds in the ground, until the Mabaso heights protected it from prying British eyes.

The army lay quietly in the valley that night, and indeed had intended to let the 22nd pass without incident. It was around the time of the new moon; a time when dark spiritual forces lurked close to the daylight world of living men, an inauspicious time to launch an assault. In any case it seems that the Zulu commanders were not yet committed to the attack. Early on the 22nd, the sound of distant firing from Mangeni brought one of the Zulu regiments out onto the iNyoni heights; the movement Pulleine had spotted from the camp. They had returned to the valley by the time Durnford made his sortie, but any hope of staying where they were was shattered as soon as Raw's horsemen appeared on the skyline above them.

Immediately, the nearest regiment, the uKhandempemvu, started up towards the horsemen, drawing those on either side after it. Raw's men fired a volley or two to slow them down, then retired towards the camp. But if the Zulu army streamed out of the valley in some confusion, their *izinduna* soon regained control, for by the time the army had

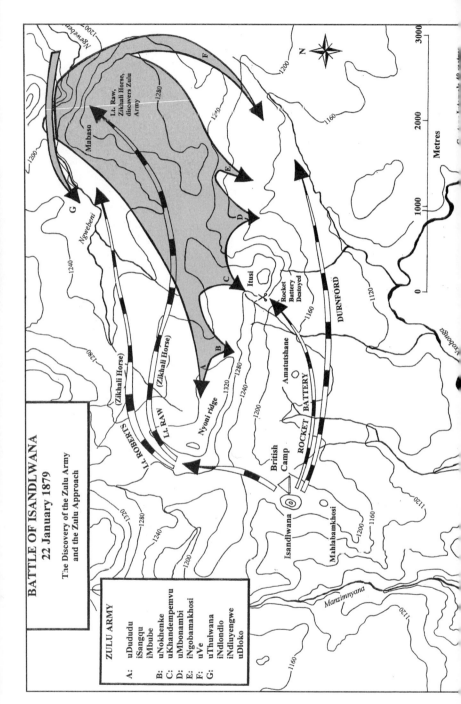

BATTLE OF ISANDLWANA
22 January 1879

The Discovery of the Zulu Army
and the Zulu Approach

ZULU ARMY

A: uDududu
iSangqu
iMbube
B: uNokhenke
C: uKhandempemvu
D: uMbonambi
E: iNgobamakhosi
F: uVe
G: uThulwana
iNdlondlo
iNdluyengwe
uDloko

Ngwebeni

Mabaso

Lt. Raw,
Zikhali Horse,
discovers Zulu
Army

F

E

D

C

B

A

G

Ngwebeni

(Zikhali Horse)

Lt. ROBERTS (Zikhali Horse)

Lt. RAW

Nyoni ridge

Itusi

Rocket
Battery
Destroyed

DURNFORD

Amatutshane

ROCKET BATTERY

British
Camp

Isandlwana

Mahlabamkhosi

Manzimnyana

N

Metres

1200
1280
1240
1200
1320
1280
1240
1200
1130
1160
1200
1160
1120
1160
1280
1240
1200

crossed the five miles of undulating country to the iNyoni escarpment, the regiments were perfectly placed. If the attack had been launched spontaneously, there can be little doubt that the Zulu commanders had already discussed contingency plans, for the Zulu dispositions revealed a thorough understanding of the British weaknesses and complete mastery of the terrain.

From the very start of the battle, it was the Zulu who retained the initiative. Colonel Pulleine, caught on the hop, not fully understanding the extent of the danger until it was too late, was left to react as best he could.

By the time the first report from Durnford's men on the heights reached Pulleine in the camp, he had already sent one company of the 1/24th, under Lieutenant Cavaye, onto the ridge. This was probably in respect of his agreement to support Durnford; the men had marched up the spur beyond Isandlwana and had disappeared over the skyline, out of sight. From his position in the camp, Pulleine could see nothing of the events on the heights, though the crackle of shots from Raw's and Roberts' troops drew nearer, and after a while Cavaye's company could be heard coming into action. Pulleine had ordered the 24th to stand to again, and they were lined up in columns in front of their tents.

For all Pulleine's personal inexperience, he must have been advised by the officers of his battalion, most of whom had been in action several times before. At this point, it seemed that the threat was coming from a specific direction – north – and Pulleine made his dispositions accordingly. He sent a further company of the 24th, under Captain Mostyn, up onto the ridge to support Cavaye, and ordered the two 7 pdr guns to take up a position on the edge of the flats in front of the camp, facing towards the slope. At this stage, no one in the camp expected the Zulu threat to be a serious one; on the Cape Frontier, such alarms had been common, but the enemy had seldom been able to mount a real attack. Besides, the prevailing opinion was that Lord Chelmsford was, at that very moment, fighting the main Zulu army a dozen miles away. Even when Mostyn's company reached the ridge and came into action beside Cavaye, firing at a long column of Zulu moving across their front down a shallow valley from right to left, the full extent of the danger was still not apparent.

Mostyn and Cavaye's position is best reached by making a short circular drive from the Visitors' Centre car park along the top of the iNyoni ridge. Take the road which leads up to your left; as you climb up the spur, you will see a stony valley on your left. Mostyn and Cavaye were formed in extended order on the slope to your left rear, with their backs to Isandlwana; the Zulu right horn was advancing across their front on the opposite side of the valley, coming from behind the high point ahead of you (Mkwene hill), and aiming for the valley behind Isandlwana. If you continue on this road, it crosses the heights, and you will reach an intersection further along the escarpment; a right turn will bring you back to Isandlwana. If you go left, you will strike the main Nquthu/Babanango road.

As you reach the top of the ridge, the road passes close to the edge, above the Isandlwana Lodge. Stop here to view the battlefield from the perspective of the Zulu commanders, who were on the rocks above the present Lodge. Their spot was well chosen; it is the only one that commands a view of the entire battlefield and is very different from Pulleine's limited perspective in the camp.

It was perhaps only when Zulu skirmishers, thrown out in front of the 'chest', reached the skyline and came into view that Pulleine realized the true extent of the Zulu assault. It was immediately apparent that Mostyn and Cavaye were isolated and in danger of being cut off. Pulleine sent a messenger to recall them; they fell back to the bottom of the slope, mixed up with the retiring black cavalry.

From their position on the Nyoni heights the companies of Mostyn and Cavaye were hidden from the camp. This photo shows their viewpoint as the right horn of the Zulu army passed from right to left before them. The fire from these two companies did little to halt the Zulu movement.

As the Zulu attack developed their commanders took up a position on the Nyoni ridge. This photo is taken from Isandlwana Lodge, which has been built directly below this position, and gives a very similar view.

At this stage, there was still time for Pulleine to organize an efficient defence. Chelmsford's Standing Orders, honed in the battles on the Cape Frontier, specified an extended infantry firing line, with guns in the middle and auxiliaries on the flanks. With the Zulu only now descending from the ridge, Pulleine attempted to form such a line. Two companies of the 1/24th, under Captain Wardell and Lieutenant Porteous, had already formed up on either side of the guns, while Mostyn, Cavaye, Raw and Roberts fell in to the left. The extreme left was anchored by Captain Younghusband's company, 1/24th, which was positioned in echelon so as to cover the retreat of Mostyn and Cavaye, while at the same time laying down fire to deny the Zulu shelter in the valley close behind the northern end of Isandlwana. The right was more problematic, and a company of the 2/24th, under Lieutenant Pope, had extended some way towards the distinctive conical koppie below the escarpment.

For the most part, the line took advantage of the terrain, with the 24th deployed along a low rocky rise, which commanded the hollows at the foot of the escarpment. As the Zulu descended the slopes, they were exposed first to shell fire from N/5's guns, and then to the 24th's

Those 24th companies forming the right half of the firing line took advantage of the terrain and deployed amongst an area of rocks and boulders, at its highest on the right of this photograph.

musketry. A line of dongas scarred the bottom of the hollows and here the Zulu attack began to falter. The warriors took what cover they could among the boulders and gullies; ahead of them lay three or four hundred yards of open ground, sloping gently up towards the British position, raked with fire and entirely devoid of cover.

While Pulleine was preoccupied with the Zulu attack to the north of the camp, Durnford had run into the right horn. His rocket battery was the first to suffer. With its troughs and ammunition boxes carried on mules, and escorted by a company of the NNC on foot, the rocket battery had lagged behind Durnford's advance and indeed Durnford had disappeared from sight, round the eastern slope of the escarpment. Warned by riders from the ridge of the Zulu approach, Major Russell directed his men to set up their equipment half-way up the slope. They had only just done so when a cloud of Zulu skirmishers, screening the advance of the iNgobamakhosi regiment, came over the skyline ahead of them. Russell's men had time to fire one rocket, which merely prompted the Zulu to stream into a nearby donga. They emerged just a few yards away and fired a volley which effectively destroyed Russell's command. Russell was killed, the mules broke away in panic and the escort and crew fled. Only the determined action of an officer of the NNC, who rallied a handful of his men, prevented the Zulu from over-running them completely.

Durnford, meanwhile, had gone perhaps four miles from the camp, hugging the foot of the ridge, when he ran into a column of the enemy, about 1,500 strong, heading straight towards him. Durnford was completely taken by surprise, but to his credit he immediately extended his mounted men in line and began a fighting retreat. Such manoeuvres were notoriously difficult under fire, especially when faced by overwhelming numbers, and it says much for Durnford's ability as a commander that he was able to keep his men under control. One of them, Jabez Molife, describes that moment:

> 'After this we remounted and retreated 20 yards, always in a long thin line, then dismounted and fired, up again for another ten yards, dismounted and fired again, and so on ten yards at a time, firing always, slowly back towards camp. We were not very many, but because of the way we were handled by our leader we were enough to stop the Zulu on that side for a long time.'

As he retreated towards the camp, Durnford picked up the survivors of the rocket battery. When they reached a deep, wide donga – the Nyogane – about a mile in front of the camp, they found it defended by some of the mounted men Chelmsford had left in camp – a mix of Natal Carbineers, Newcastle Mounted Rifles and Buffalo Border Guard, in all fifty-two men under Captain Bradstreet of the NMR Durnford's men spilled into the donga beside them and dismounted. Leaving their horses in the bottom, they lined the forward lip, firing at the Zulu streaming down behind them.

The Zulu attack was now fully developed. On the extreme left, the left horn – the uVe *ibutho*, the youngest in the army – had been pursuing Durnford, followed closely by the slightly older

When Colonel Durnford's command was forced to retire by the Zulu left, he took up a position in this donga, or dry watercourse, on the extreme right of the British position.

Durnford's position was about a mile in front of the British camp. This photo gives an idea of the distance it was necessary for his men to ride in the fruitless search to find their ammunition wagon in the confusion of the camp.

iNgobamakhosi. So heavy was the fire from the donga that the uVe faltered and went to ground and did not advance again until the iNgobamakhosi came up to support them. Even so, they were only able to rise up and make short rushes before throwing themselves down in the long grass again.

To the right of the left horn were the uMbonambi and uKhandempemvu regiments, who stretched in a long arc from below the conical hill, round to the spur. On the right of the uKhandempemvu, the uNokhenke had followed up Mostyn and Cavaye with such enthusiasm that they had suffered heavily from the fire from Younghusband's men and had been forced to retire back over the skyline. Further right still, the right horn – the uDududu, iSangqu and iMbube regiments – had slipped into the valley behind Isandlwana. The famous 'chest and horns' formation required one horn to remain hidden by the ground if possible, and now these regiments slowly worked their way down the valley, concealing themselves in the long grass.

At this point it still looked as if the British might win the battle. One survivor, Lieutenant Horace Smith-Dorrien, recalled that the 24th were,

> '... no boy recruits, but war-worn men, and fresh from the old colony where they had carried everything before them. Possessed of a splendid discipline and sure of success, they lay on their position making every round tell ...'

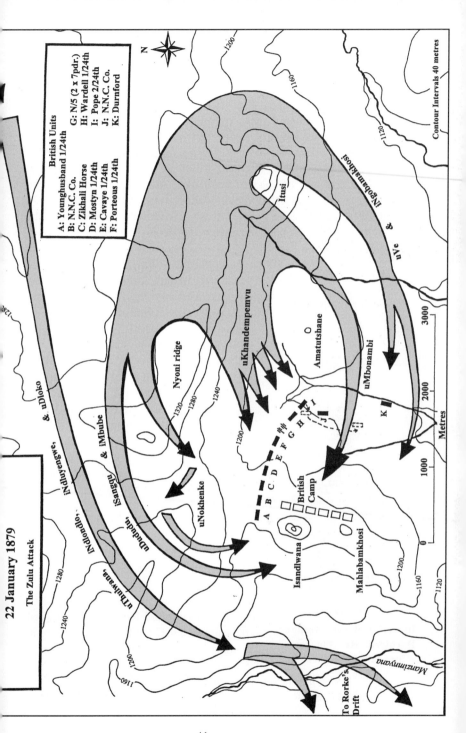

22 January 1879

The Zulu Attack

British Units

A: Younghusband 1/24th
B: N.N.C. Co.
C: Zikhali Horse
D: Mostyn 1/24th
E: Cavaye 1/24th
F: Porteous 1/24th
G: N/5 (2 x 7pdr.)
H: Wardell 1/24th
I: Pope 2/24th
J: N.N.C. Co.
K: Durnford

Contour Intervals 40 metres

N

iNyoni ridge

ukhandempemvu

Amatutshane

uMbonambi

iNdlondlo,

iNdluyengwe,
& uDloko

iSangqu
& iMbube

uDududu

uThulwana,

uNokhenke

British Camp

Isandlwana

Mahlabamkhosi

Itusi

iNcobamakhosi

uVe

To Rorke's
Drift

Manzinnyana

Metres

0   1000   2000   3000

A warrior named uMhoti of the uKhandempemvu was on the receiving end of that fire:

'... the soldiers who lay on the flat ground in front of the camp poured volley after volley into the *impi*; we crouched down, and dare not advance.'

Yet this impression was deeply misleading. On the right, Durnford might have been in his element, cheering his men on as they drove the left horn back, but in fact his position was acutely vulnerable. The nearest company of redcoats was Pope's, which was several hundred yards away to the left, and more daring elements of the uMbonambi were already slipping between the two, with only a company of the NNC further back preventing them threatening the camp. In front of him the uVe and iNgobamakhosi were extending to their left and were threatening to outflank him further down-stream. Moreover, Durnford's men were running low on ammunition and when he sent riders into the camp to search for more supplies, they could not find where his wagons had been parked.

It was at this point, quite suddenly, that the British position collapsed. Pulleine, remembering his promise to support Durnford and worried about his over-extended right, ordered Pope to swing round to the right in an attempt to block the gap. Pope's company had just begun the movement when Durnford abandoned the donga and fell back. A staff officer met him as he rode in, and recalled,

'He had, I think, already observed the state of affairs, and was looking very serious. He asked me if I could bring some men to keep the enemy in check in our rear.'

In fact, Pulleine had no men to spare. It is possible that Durnford found him somewhere in the camp and together they decided to retire the whole line, to take up a position closer to the tents. According to uMhoti,

Brevet Colonel Anthony Durnford, RE, the senior officer killed at Isandlwana.

'Then, at the sound of a bugle, the firing ceased at a breath, and the whole force rose from the ground and retired on the tents. Like a flame the whole Zulu force sprang to its feet and darted upon them ...'

In fact, the Zulu attack had been deliberately launched by Ntshingwayo. Watching from the lip of the escarpment, he had seen the Zulu centre pinned down under British fire, and had sent one of his *izinduna* – Mkhosana kaMvundlana, a Chief of the Biyela, who held a command in the uKhandempemvu – down to urge them forward. In an incident which has passed into Zulu folklore, Mkhosana strode among the prostrate warriors of the uKhandempemvu, berating them, and evoking the praises of King Cetshwayo to inspire them. Mkhosana was killed shortly after but deserves to be remembered as one of the great Zulu heroes of the battle. The uKhandempemvu rose to the challenge just as Pulleine began his retreat. Far out on the Zulu left, the *izinduna* of the iNgobamakhosi – great rivals of the uKhandempemvu – saw the fresh attack and challenged their own men. 'Why are you lying down?' called Sikizane kaNomageje to his men, 'What was it you said to the uKhandempemvu? There are the uKhandempemvu going into the tents... Stop firing. Go in hand to hand!'

The sudden rush was an awesome spectacle and too much for many of the auxiliary units, who suddenly seemed dangerously exposed. While the 24th companies retreated in good order, stopping every few yards to fire, the NNC moved much quicker. Gaps appeared in the British line, and the Zulu rushed between them, preventing the 24th from forming a united body. One NNC officer, whose men had been held in reserve in front of the tents, recalled the sudden panic which swept through them:

'... as [the Zulu] got on the right flank they made a rush for the camp, and drove back the few men that opposed them, when my company saw them coming on, nothing could stop them, they all jumped up and ran and though I knocked a man down with my rifle it was no use. I then saw the men of the 2nd Batt. N.N.C. running and looking for the 24th men, I saw that they were retreating also, but very slowly. All the mounted men were riding past as fast as they could ...'

By the time the 24th reached the tents, the fighting was raging hand to hand. On the extreme left, Younghusband's company had retired up the slope along the face of the hill and had taken up a commanding position on a shoulder of Isandlwana itself. Here they were able to keep the Zulu at bay, until their ammunition dwindled, and they found themselves effectively trapped. Below them, the 24th tried to rally together, between Isandlwana and the ridge to the south. Here, however, they were attacked from the rear by the right horn, which rushed up from the valley behind the mountain to complete the encirclement. A Zulu recalled this desperate struggle:

'They were completely surrounded on all side, and stood back to back; and surrounding some men who were in the centre. Their ammunition was now done, except that they had some revolvers which they fired at us at close quarters. We were unable to break their square until we had killed a good many of them, by throwing our assegais at short distances. We eventually overcame them all in this way.'

Durnford himself had joined a group of colonial volunteers who were trying to hold back the Zulu left. Mehlokazulu, Sihayo's son, who held a junior command with the iNgobamakhosi, described their end:

Mehlokazulu kaSihayo. The senior son of a prominent chief in the Isandlwana district, he fought during the battle with the iNgobamakhosi regiment. After the war he was arrested by the British but released without charge.

'It was a long time before they were overcome – before we finished them. When we did get to them, they died all in one place together. They threw down their guns when their ammunition was done, and then commenced with their pistols, which they used as long as their ammunition lasted; and then they formed a line, shoulder to shoulder and back to back, and fought with their knives ...'

Later, Mehlokazulu saw their bodies clumped together, and in the centre 'a dead officer with his arm in a sling and a big moustache'.

On the shoulder of the mountain, Younghusband had at last realized the hopelessness of his position and led his men in a dashing bayonet charge, in an attempt to join the surviving knots of 24th. Perhaps he succeeded; the biggest clump of 24th dead was later found on the nek below the crag, and someone claimed to recognize

44

Many groups of redcoats were overwhelmed as they were driven back through the camp area.

both Younghusband and Pulleine among them.

As the Zulu streamed through the tents, killing everything they could, nature itself added an apocalyptic touch; there was a partial eclipse, and the moon passed across the face of the sun. As one warrior put it, 'the sun turned black in the middle of the battle'.

Some elements of the 24th succeeded in retiring over the nek and into the valley of the Manzimnyana stream beyond, probably hoping to retire towards Rorke's Drift. The pressure from the right horn, however, forced them off the road and down among the boulders and dongas which scar the valley sides. Many fought all the way; Lieutenant Anstey and a party of his men were only overcome on the banks of the stream itself. Many individuals fought on from behind the slender cover of trees or boulders, prolonging their final moments. One man retired up the slopes of Isandlwana itself and defended a cave at the foot of the cliffs, until at last a group of warriors fired into the cave and killed him. Behind the heroic imagery of this dogged resistance lies a grim truth; that the men on foot were trapped, and had nowhere else to go.

As soon as the line collapsed, a stream of men – auxiliaries, camp personnel, civilian wagon drivers – tried to escape. The lucky ones managed to pass between the Zulu horns before they closed, but they faced a harrowing flight across country with the Zulu in pursuit. Their route took them down the Manzimnyama, then up Mpethe hill beyond, and finally into the valley of the Mzinyathi – the border with Natal. The two guns of N/5 battery had managed to escape the carnage in the camp, but stuck fast in the broken country beyond the nek and were overtaken. Most of the men on foot were exhausted by the time they reached Mpethe and the greatest slaughter occurred in the Manzimnyama valley. A fresh horror awaited those who reached the river, for elements of the Zulu reserve – the uThulwana, iNdluyengwe,

A stirring representation of Lieutenant Melvill's attempt to escape with the cased Queen's Colour of his battalion.

iNdlondlo and uDloko regiments, who had taken no part hitherto in the fight – swung across country and caught them above the river. The river itself was in flood and many of the fugitives had no choice but to plunge in; many were drowned.

In the closing moments of the camp, Lieutenant Melvill, adjutant of the 1/24th, had taken the Queen's Colour of his battalion, probably in the hope of rallying his men. It was too late, however, for the battalion had disintegrated and instead Melvill tried to carry the Colour to safety. Along the way he met Lieutenant Coghill, of Glyn's staff, and together the two reached the river. Mid-way across the river, however, the current tore the Colour from Melvill's grasp and it was swept away downstream. The two men staggered onto the Natal bank and dragged themselves half-way up the slopes beyond. Here, they were overtaken and killed; they were among the last British soldiers to die in the battle.

Once the Zulu had flushed out and destroyed the last pockets of resistance, they looted the camp, carrying away a thousand Martini-Henry rifles and hundreds of thousands of rounds of ammunition. At least a thousand Zulu were killed in the battle, and their friends and relatives dragged the bodies into dongas or grain pits, or simply left

Fugitives' drift on the Mzinyathi (Buffalo River). Those fleeing from the battle descended from the high ground on the right and attempted to cross the flooded river to the Natal bank. Melvill and Coghill successfully crossed the river but were pursued and killed.

The death of Lieutenants Melvill and Coghill.

Melvill and Coghill's grave.

them lying, covered by their own war shields. Hundreds more warriors had suffered appalling injuries from the heavy calibre British bullets and faced long, painful journeys to their homes to recover. Many did not make it. In accordance with their religious beliefs, the warriors partially stripped the bodies of the dead British and slashed open the stomach of each corpse; the bodies were left where they fell. By late afternoon, the army had begun to retire to the Ngwebeni.

In the early evening, Chelmsford returned to the camp. He had found no Zulu at Mangeni; at last the trickle of odd reports emanating from Isandlwana had convinced him to return. He found his camp destroyed, his tents on fire, and the bodies of more than 1,300 of his men – black and white – strewn among the debris, mixed up with the carcasses of hundreds of oxen, horses and mules, killed in the fury of the Zulu attack.

And more bad news awaited him. As he reached the nek and looked out towards the

Natal border, the outline of Shiyane hill was silhouetted by fire. The post at Rorke's Drift was under attack.

The morning after; Lord Chelmsford's men retreat from a scene of utter devastation.

Today, the area immediately around Isandlwana camp is a protected site enabling the visitor to explore it at leisure. A good view of the battlefield as a whole can be obtained from the slopes of the ridge to the south of Isandlwana, known to the Zulu as Mahlabamkhosi, and to the British as Black's Kopje. Looking straight across at the mountain in front of you, the camp was on the right, along the foot of the mountain; the Zulu attack developed from the ridge beyond. To your right, across the plain, the roof of a clinic and a clump of trees, marks the site of the Nyogane donga, roughly where Durnford defended it. The piles of whitewashed cairns mark British graves, and the story of the fight can be read in them; they are scattered thinly on the firing line, but cluster together as the troops were driven back

Isandlwana, photographed in September 1879. Broken wagons, debris and the skeletons of animals and men still litter the site.

The cluster of cairns and monuments on the nek between Isandlwana and Mahlabamkhosi confirm the ferocity of the fighting in this area.

A view of the nek, from the slopes of Isandlwana. The large cluster of cairns in the centre marks the last stand of colonial troops, among whose bodies was found that of Colonel Durnford. At the time of the battle the track passed on the nearside of the cairns. The large cairn in the foreground commemorates the stand of Captain Younghusband's company, 1/24th.

through the tents. The greatest concentration is on the nek; they then spill out to your left, marking the line of retreat down the so-called 'fugitives' trail'. The large cairn directly below you marks the site of one major concentration of bodies; the site of another is marked by the 24th memorial. To your right, a cluster of monuments by the side of the road marks the site of Durnford's last stand; his body was later exhumed and buried in Fort Napier cemetery, Pietermaritzburg. Another clump of cairns on the rear slope of Isandlwana – to your left

A line of cairns on the Fugitives' Trail. The groups of cairns on the trail suggest that elements of organized British resistance lasted as far as the Manzimnyana stream.

The new memorial to the Zulu dead, erected in 1999. The design is based on the *iziqu*, the traditional bravery bead necklace.

– mark an attempt to hold back the right horn, possibly by elements of the NNC, led by Captain Shepstone.

Many of the Zulu dead were buried in the dongas between the battlefield gateway and the Visitors' Centre. A new memorial by the gate, shaped like a giant iziqu 'bravery bead' necklace, commemorates their sacrifice. Many Zulu bones were exposed in these dongas over the last century, and they were gathered together by the missionaries at St. Vincent's and re-interred behind the church; a small chapel now marks the spot.

It is possible to walk the 'fugitives' trail', but this is best attempted with a local guide. It's a difficult walk, easy to get lost, and it is often necessary to swim the river at the far end. For those less energetic, the graves of Lieutenants Melvill and Coghill can be reached by car from Rorke's Drift.

Chapter Three

Coastal Column – Caught in the Open

If the perennial interest in the dramatic events at Isandlwana and Rorke's Drift is understandable, it has nonetheless served to overshadow the story of another battle, equally fascinating in its way, which was fought elsewhere in Zululand that very same day. Away to the south of these two famous clashes Colonel Pearson's No. 1 Column was caught in the open by an *impi* led by Godide kaNdlela at the Battle of Nyezane. By the end of the battle the British soldiers had learnt a new respect for their Zulu opponents.

As we have already seen Lord Chelmsford's plan of campaign called for three invasion columns, with another two employed in a defensive role on the border. Colonel Charles Knight Pearson commanded the right hand column of this invasion force, known as No.1 Column or the Coastal Column. Pearson had come out to South Africa with his regiment, the 2nd Battalion 3rd Regiment, 'The Buffs', in 1876 and had been appointed Commandant of Natal. As Chelmsford began to organize his invasion force Pearson retired from 'The Buffs' on half-pay and joined the Staff, being handed command of No. 1 Column.

Officers of the 3rd Regiment, 'The Buffs', photographed in South Africa. Colonel Pearson, who commanded the Right Flank Column, is in civilian dress, seated left.   Canterbury Museum

The ultimatum that had been read to the Zulu delegation in December 1878 had been delivered under the wide spreading branches of a wild fig tree that grew close to the bank of the Thukela river. This spot also marked one of the old river crossing points from Natal into Zululand. The Lower Drift, as it was known, had featured much in the turbulent history of this region of Zululand and was about to feature again as it had been selected as the formation point for Pearson's column. The sham of the ultimatum was obvious, as plans had already been drafted to construct a defensive position on a high bluff overlooking the drift. By the time the ultimatum was delivered the position was completed, named Fort Pearson and manned by a naval brigade from HMS *Active* armed with two 12pdr Armstrong guns, two rocket tubes and a Gatling gun.

During the thirty days allowed to Cetshwayo, the Zulu king, to agree to the impossible demands of the ultimatum, Pearson began to build his column up to strength. There was no pretence among the British military that the invasion would not take place. By the time he was ready to begin his advance Pearson had under his command two imperial infantry battalions, his old regiment the 2nd Battalion 3rd Regiment (eight companies – 749 men) and the 99th (Duke of Edinburgh's) Regiment (six companies – 515 men); two Royal Artillery 7-pdrs and a rocket trough from 11/7 battery (26 men – the rest of the battery were with Wood's No. 4 Column.); No 2 Company, Royal Engineers (103); a Naval Brigade from HMS *Active* and HMS *Tenedos* with two 7-pdrs, two rocket tubes and a Gatling gun (290 men); a squadron of Imperial Mounted Infantry and five of the mounted Natal Volunteer Corps (total 312 mounted men); two battalions of the 2nd Regiment Natal Native Contingent (2,152 men) and No.2 Company Natal Native Pioneer Corps (104 men). With 20 men attached to the Staff and Departments, Pearson could muster 4271 fighting men. The majority of this force were in camp by 11th January 1879, the day the ultimatum expired. With no word coming from Cetshwayo, the following day Pearson commenced crossing the river into Zululand.

The site of Fort Pearson is the ideal place to begin your tour of the main sites in the coastal region. It is the easiest of all the areas of Zulu War activity to visit as it is within easy driving distance of Durban. Leaving Durban drive north, initially on the N2, before turning off at Stanger on to the R102. As you will be close to Stanger you may wish to take a quick detour into town where you will find the memorial to

Fort Pearson, built on a natural stronghold above the Thukela river, was the anchor for Pearson's advance.

The view from the site of Fort Pearson; the Lower Drift of the Thukela river, marking the border between Zululand and Natal.

One of the defensive trenches ringing the fortified bluff known as Fort Pearson. The fort became the focal point for the formation of Colonel Pearson's No.1 Column.

The landing party from HMS *Active*, photographed at the Lower Thukela. The Royal Marines are in the centre with the sailors on either flank. The Gatling gun used at Nyezane can be seen towards the right.

King Shaka, the founder of the Zulu nation. The memorial stands on the site of his Dukuza homestead, where he was assassinated in 1828. Continuing north on the R102 you will come to signs indicating a right turn to the Harold Johnson Nature Reserve and Fort Pearson. Continue to follow the Fort Pearson signs and you will come to a small parking and picnic area by the Euphorbia Hill redoubt site or, if you continue along the track, you will reach a parking area on the lower slopes of the bluff on which Fort Pearson stands. Euphorbia Hill now contains the graves of a number of soldiers who died of disease during

Naval Brigade troops with a Gatling gun man the central redoubt at the Fort Pearson complex, January 1879.

the Zulu War. Sadly their names are lost from the graves, each plot now poignantly marked with a simple whitewashed headstone bearing the words 'Here Rests A Brave British Soldier'. However, there is one marked grave here, that of Captain Warren Wynne, Commander of No. 2 Company RE. It was Wynne who was to be the architect of the impressive defences of Pearson's fort at Eshowe. Although struck down by disease at Eshowe, Wynne survived the siege and was brought down to Fort Pearson where he hung on to life for another couple of weeks, before he finally passed away on his thirty-sixth birthday.

The trenches and ramparts of Fort Pearson are well preserved and give a good impression of what an impossible task it would have been for the Zulu if they had attempted to storm it. The view from here of the gently rolling green hills is typical of the coastal region and if your

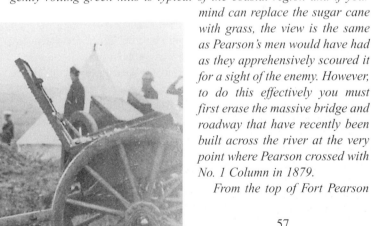

mind can replace the sugar cane with grass, the view is the same as Pearson's men would have had as they apprehensively scoured it for a sight of the enemy. However, to do this effectively you must first erase the massive bridge and roadway that have recently been built across the river at the very point where Pearson crossed with No. 1 Column in 1879.

From the top of Fort Pearson

there is a path that leads down the side of the bluff, follows a footbridge across the new road and finally deposits you on the riverbank. Dwarfed by the supports of the bridge over the river, you are now standing a mere arm's length from history. For here, caged, stands a withered stump, all that remains today of the wild fig tree under which the ultimatum was read to the Zulu ambassadors in December 1878.

Pearson's orders were quite straightforward. He was to advance as rapidly as possible to the abandoned Norwegian Mission at Eshowe, some thirty-five miles by the solitary winding trader's track. Eshowe had been selected as it was known that there were buildings at the mission station. These would be extremely useful, for Chelmsford wanted to establish a major supply dump here. Pearson's orders were that he should unload his first convoy of wagons, entrench the position and having established a garrison, send the wagons back to the border where they were to be reloaded before returning to Eshowe once more. In the meantime a second convoy of wagons was to be held in readiness to move up to Eshowe once Pearson had safely made the first trip. Pearson was not to advance beyond Eshowe until the Left and Centre Columns had made significant progress towards oNdini, Cetshwayo's principal homestead.

Although the first of Pearson's men crossed the Thukela at dawn on 12th January it was not until late the following day that everyone was safely across the river. A garrison of naval personnel and some of the Natal Native Contingent were left to man Fort Pearson. However, although all the men were across the river it still took another three days before the last of the supplies and wagons were hauled over. It was therefore only on the evening of 16th January that Pearson could finally say he was ready to begin his advance. The following day was spent finalizing plans and organizing the order of march. Then at 3.30am on 18th January the bugles sounded and the men of No.1 Column emerged from their tents into a cold, rainy pre-dawn and prepared to move off. At last Pearson was on the move.

Having carefully considered the effect the recent heavy rains would have on the track, Pearson elected to split his force into two separate divisions for the march to Eshowe. He would accompany the first division himself. This would consist of fifty wagons escorted by all eight companies of the 2/3rd, the Royal Artillery, the Royal Engineers, part of the landing party from HMS *Active* with their guns and rockets, seven companies of the 1st Battalion 2nd NNC, a half company of the Natal Native Pioneers, the Mounted Infantry and three of the mounted

Natal Volunteer Corps. They were to start twenty-four hours in advance of the second division and march to the Nyoni river, push across and make camp between that river and the next, the mSundusi. It proved a difficult task as the passage of the wagons over the track soon reduced it to a morass and the crossing of the Nyoni proved to be more testing than anticipated. After an exhausting day and with the return of the rain in the afternoon, Pearson was forced to make camp on the far bank of the Nyoni.

The difficulties he had experienced the previous day persuaded Pearson to wait for the second division to come up. He realized that this part of his force would be hampered even more than he had been by the state of the track and would certainly not be able to reach the mSundusi, which he had hoped would be possible. Instead he decided that his division would sit out the morning at the Nyoni while the second division moved up, continued on to the mSundusi in the afternoon and made camp there.

The second division was placed under the command of Lieutenant-Colonel Welman, 99th Regiment, and was charged with the responsibility of escorting eighty wagons up to Eshowe. Welman's division was weaker than that led by Pearson, having only two companies of the 99th Regiment, the 2nd Battalion 2nd NNC, the other half company of the Natal Native Pioneers and one of the Natal Volunteer Corps. After the safe completion of the first day's march Pearson planned to transfer three companies of 'The Buffs' to augment their numbers.

The cemetery today at Euphorbia Hill redoubt, close to Fort Pearson. Captain Wynne, RE., the architect of the fort at Eshowe is buried here. There are two cemeteries in the area where those soldiers and sailors who died of disease during the campaign were buried. Each is marked with the poignant inscription 'Here rests a brave British soldier'.

Welman's division had a hellish journey to the Nyoni. The track was now in a wretched condition and it was only by the application of many shoulders to the wheels that the convoy edged forward at all. As they approached the Nyoni with thoughts that the day's toil was almost over, the struggling, muddied soldiers of the second division were greeted with the sight of the refreshed and rested first division resuming their march with the orders that they were to cross the Nyoni and follow on. Pearson's division made good progress, reached the mSundusi, brought all their wagons over and made camp a short distance beyond the river. Welman's men did the best they could. About thirty of his wagons crossed to the far bank of the mSundusi, twenty more reached the river but could not cross, while the final thirty were left to struggle in on their own, unguarded. Welman's men all crossed to the new camp for the night except one solitary company of the 99th who were ordered to protect the fifty wagons that had otherwise been left to their own devices. It is clear that at this point in the campaign the British Army generally disregarded the Zulu as a dangerous enemy. Pearson had received intelligence from a Border Agent during the day that an *impi* had been dispatched to attack him, yet he made no attempt to form an organized laager as prescribed in the Field Force Regulations and Welman's wagon convoy was left largely unguarded and spread out across country.

In fact the information Pearson had received was largely accurate. Some 3,500 men, under the command of the seventy year old Godide kaNdlela, had been sent from oNdini to the coastal sector to join the local forces, with the intention of halting Pearson's advance. It was lucky for Pearson and his men that on this night Godide was still too far away to take advantage of this lapse in British discipline.

To the great relief of the majority of soldiers who had pushed, pulled, slipped and slithered their way to the mSundusi, Colonel Pearson decided to hold his position on 20th January, sending a large work party ahead to prepare the drift at the next river crossing, the amaTigulu.

The slow advance recommenced on the morning of 21st January, this time the second division followed directly behind the first. Pearson received more intelligence which told of the possibility of a large Zulu force of between 4,000 – 5,000 men positioned about five miles to the east, near a large *ikhanda*, or military homestead, known as kwaGingindlovu. Pearson sent a detachment of about 400 infantry, naval personnel, artillery and mounted men with 200 black auxiliaries to investigate. The *ikhanda* was deserted except for an old crone who was taken and the huts burnt down. There was no sign of the rumoured Zulu force, but it was close. By nightfall they were in the area and watching the new British camp just beyond the river. Godide considered launching an attack that night but, unsure of the terrain, concerned about his ability to control the attack in the dark and unnerved by the calls of the camp sentries, he chose instead to withdraw. He moved northwards and took up a position in the hills beyond the Nyezane river, the next obstacle in Pearson's path.

The 22nd January, a momentous day in the annals of the British Army, dawned with a crisp chill in the air. Even before the dramatic events at Isandlwana and Rorke's Drift had begun to unfold, Pearson's column was in action. At 4.00am a body of mounted men was sent ahead to scout the bush either side of the track, looking for any sign of the enemy. The bush was declared clear and at 4.30am the first division, with its precious convoy of wagons, lumbered forward. The advance was slow due to the poor state of the track and the Royal Engineers and Natal Native Pioneers were constantly at work to keep it open for the passage of the wagons. Eventually the leading mounted men reached the Nyezane, crossed the river and found themselves on a fairly flat expanse of open ground beyond which the track turned and began to climb a range of hills. Although the area was surrounded by bush there was water present and with the prospect of hard work ahead

The Nyezane river. Pearson's column had crossed the river and was preparing to climb the range of hills in the background when Zulu appeared on Wombane, the right hand hill. The ensuing battle ended in victory for the British.

Wombane

Wombane hill. The left horn of the Zulu army was stung into a premature attack by the advance of a company of the NNC. In response Pearson anchored his position on this knoll on the central spur of the range.

climbing the hills, it was decided to halt the column here for a couple of hours to rest the oxen. Vedettes were posted and those mounted men not required for this duty were given permission to fall out while the column slowly edged forward to the designated spot.

The route of the track ahead ran up the crest of a spur, which extended down from the high ground above. On either side of the spur the land dropped steeply into bush-choked ravines before rising again to higher spurs, running parallel with the track. The spur on the right led up to the dominating hilltop of Wombane. With the first wagons now crawling into the rest camp, a vedette rode in with news that he had observed a small group of Zulu on the hills ahead. Pearson reacted by sending a company of the NNC forward with orders to drive this small group away. The black auxiliaries, led by their white officers and NCOs, advanced with spirit along the track and as they began to climb they observed the group of Zulu on the skyline ahead. However, almost instantly they melted away into the bush, before reappearing on the slope of the Wombane spur. The NNC, following their orders to drive the Zulu away, likewise descended into the ravine and reformed on the lower Wombane slopes. Their elusive quarry had disappeared again but the NNC officers ordered their men forward, up the slope of Wombane, towards the last position the Zulu had occupied. The men began to move but they were not happy; something was wrong. A number of the men detected a low murmur from the long grass ahead and feared an ambush, but they could not make their officers and NCOs understand. Moments later the silence was shattered when from the long grass to their front several hundred fully armed warriors leapt into view with a great cry of 'uSuthu!' and unleashed a ragged volley from their antiquated firearms. The men of the NNC turned and ran but a group of officers and NCOs attempted to make a stand. It was a futile gesture for which they paid with their lives. The Zulu swept down upon them and after a brief struggle they were overrun.

The men who had been acting as vedettes, the Mounted Infantry and Natal Hussars, immediately fell back, reformed and then dismounted, taking up a position to the right of the track. Eight of their number who were too far off drew together on the left of the three spurs. The mounted men of the Victoria and Stanger Mounted Rifles who had fallen out, rushed for their horses and returned to the track from where they were ordered to form to its left, facing the high ground. No sooner were they in position than Zulu appeared on the high ground to their front. One of the Volunteers later wrote,

'... every hillside was swarming with them. Down they came, rushing on to us, and defiling as to surround us, disappearing into bushy ravines below, soon to be seen swarming over the next ridge nearer to us, and preparing to rush down it and close with us.'

Pearson, who was on the flat grassy area at the foot of the hills when the attack began, was ideally positioned to issue his orders. Just to the right of the track as it began to ascend the centre spur was a knoll that offered a good view of Wombane. Pearson chose this point on which to anchor his position. The first two companies of 'The Buffs', the Royal Artillery and the Naval Brigade were ordered to pass between the two bodies of mounted men at the double and take up position on the knoll. Immediately they reached the position, the two Royal Artillery 7-pdrs swung into action and added their fire to that of the two Buffs companies which was directed against the Zulu streaming down from Wombane. Among the Zulu on the receiving end of this concentration of fire was Chief Zimema of the uMxhapho *ibutho*. He later told of his experiences during the battle:

'We were told to advance and, grasping our arms ... we went

forward packed close together like a lot of bees ... we were still far away from them when the white men began to throw their bullets at us, but we could not shoot at them because our rifles would not shoot so far ... When we were near them we opened fire, hitting a number of them ... After that they brought out their 'by-and-by' [artillery] and we heard what we thought was a long pipe [rocket] coming towards us. As we advanced we had our rifles under our arms and had our assegais in our right hands ready to throw them, but they were not much good for we never got near enough to use them. We never got nearer than 50 paces to the English, and although we tried to climb over our fallen brothers we could not get very far ahead because the white men were firing heavily close to the ground into our front ranks while the 'by-and-by' was firing over our heads into the regiments behind us... The battle was so fierce that we had to wipe the blood and brains of the killed and wounded from our heads, faces, arms, legs and shields after the fighting.'

Leaving Fort Pearson return to the main road, turn right and head northwards crossing the Thukela river. At the junction with the R68 turn left following the signs towards Eshowe. After a short distance you will pass the sign to Gingindlovu battlefield, the road passing through the centre of the British position at that battle as it reaches the high ground. As you continue on this road the hills that form the backdrop to the Battle of Nyezane come into view. Just before the road begins to climb, a sign directing you to Nyezane will take you off the main road to the left. Follow this dirt road for a short distance, about 100 metres or so, until you reach a junction. The hill that you have just passed directly on your right is the knoll where Pearson moved his artillery and infantry. Leave your vehicle by the junction and take the track up towards the knoll and a few metres further on you will find the modern memorial that marks the site where the British casualties were buried. Continue up the track and by taking one of the narrow paths to your right through the sugar cane you will come to a position where you will have a perfect view of Wombane, over the modern road. It was a position such as this that 'The Buffs' and artillery occupied when firing at the Zulu of the left horn as they streamed down the slopes of Wombane. As you descend from the knoll back to your vehicle, you will see traces of a dirt track extending towards the river ahead, which is itself marked by a line of low bush. This track more or less follows that used by Pearson as he advanced to the battle. Before leaving the site,

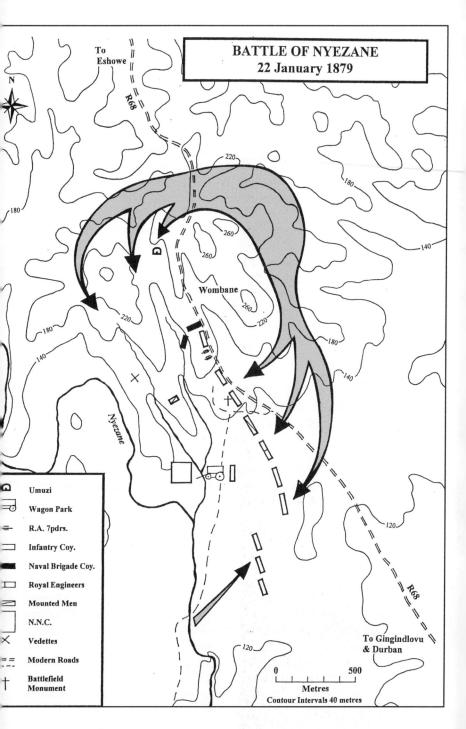

BATTLE OF NYEZANE
22 January 1879

To Eshowe

R68

N

220
180
140
260
260
Wombane
260
220
220
180
180
140
140
Nyezane
120
120

R68

To Gingindlovu
& Durban

G   Umuzi

     Wagon Park

=   R.A. 7pdrs.

     Infantry Coy.

     Naval Brigade Coy.

     Royal Engineers

     Mounted Men

     N.N.C.

X   Vedettes

= = Modern Roads

†   Battlefield
     Monument

0   500
Metres
Contour Intervals 40 metres

65

by crossing the extremely busy main road and moving a few metres up the track opposite, you can look back and enjoy a view of the knoll and the British position as the left horn would have seen it. If you can ignore the intrusion of the noisy road with its heavy traffic, which cuts a swathe through the green seas of sugar cane that flow over every hill and field, the site is largely similar to how it looked at the time of the battle. The road has altered the lie of the land a little but it is possible to follow all stages of the battle from a position on the knoll. There is even an umuzi conveniently positioned further up the slope leading from the knoll that helps complete your image of the battlefield.

It was clear as more Zulu came into view that the body on Wombane was the left horn of the Zulu attack. Another company of 'The Buffs' doubled up and was placed at the foot of the knoll, extended towards the Natal Hussars and Mounted Infantry. Despite the weight of fire directed at them, the left horn continued to advance and succeeded in getting into the bush at the foot of the slope and skirmishing through the cover they had gained, they attempted to push on towards the wagons that were still slowly crossing the river. Captain Wynne's Engineer company had been working at the river crossing when the firing started. Wynne formed his men up and pushed up the track. In an account of the battle Wynne wrote,

'The heights seemed swarming with Zulu, who were also showing signs of working round the right flank so as to get at the wagons. I therefore determined to leave the road, and turned off to the right, and having reached a low narrow ridge, where I found the Mounted Infantry posted (on foot), I extended my company in skirmishing order from their (Mounted Infantry) right. We no sooner showed ourselves on the further slope of this ridge than the Zulu, who were concealed in bush 150 to 250 yards off, began firing at us, bullets whizzing close by, right and left.'

Wynne had made a timely intervention. Now as the length of the wagon column reduced, more men could be freed to join the battle. Two companies of 'The Buffs' that had been bringing wagons in were ordered into line to the right of Wynne's engineers. Behind them the Royal Marines of the Naval Brigade, who had been marching with the Gatling gun, came forward in support. Unable to get to grips with the Zulu due to the thick bush, the naval party returned to the track and advanced to the knoll where they joined the rest of their brigade. Once in position the Gatling opened a devastating fire on a group of Zulu on

A romanticized – but otherwise largely accurate – representation of Midshipman Coker commanding the Gatling at Nyezane.

Wombane, scattering them into the open where they were picked off with rifle fire. A sixth company of Buffs remained to guard the wagons with the NNC. Lieutenant-Colonel Welman, who was pushing on with the second division as fast as he could, sent forward a half company each from 'The Buffs' and 99th to join the battle.

While the extended British line had been skirmishing with the leading elements of the left horn on the flat, up on the knoll the position had been exposed to quite a hot fire. There was no cover on the knoll and although most of the Zulu fire was largely inaccurate, the

The height of the battle, from much the same position as the photo opposite, with the burning homestead, left, and Wombane, right.

volume of it against the tightly packed British ranks was causing concern. Pearson even had his horse shot from under him. In addition to those Zulu on Wombane another fire was now directed against the knoll from part of the Zulu chest, which had taken up a position around an *umuzi* about 300 yards higher up the centre spur. From here yet another body of Zulu was attempting to extend, forming the right horn, but appeared to lack the determination shown by those on the left. Coming under fire first from the Natal Volunteers who had been formed to the left of the track, those who passed through it ran into the fire of the handful of vedettes positioned out on the left of the three spurs. It proved enough to persuade these reluctant warriors from continuing with their course of action. Back on the knoll one of the 24-pound rockets was launched at the *umuzi* harbouring the Zulu centre. With a certain amount of luck this erratic weapon passed straight

The British position on the knoll at the battle of Nyezane. The line was formed to the right of the photo, overlooking the modern road.

A view of the British position at Nyezane from the summit of Wombane. The small circular *umuzi* overlooking the road marks the knoll occupied by Pearson's command.

The British graves at Nyezane. The cross was carved by one of the Eshowe garrison, and put in place when the column withdrew in April. S.Bourquin

through the collection of circular thatched huts turning them into a flaming inferno.

Welman, meanwhile, had brought the head of his column up to the rear of the first division. Thus he was able to release his remaining one and a half companies of Buffs and a half company of the 99th to join the action. They crossed the river and formed to the right of the extended line, but the tide had turned and the Zulu were clearly pulling back towards Wombane. On the knoll too it was becoming obvious that the Zulu attack was spent, although the enemy were lingering, reluctant to retreat. Commander Campbell, who led the Naval Brigade, sought permission from Pearson to lead an attack against the burning *umuzi* where large numbers of Zulu were still formed. Pearson agreed and Campbell stormed forward with one and a half companies of his sailors, supported by a company of Buffs. Lieutenant Lloyd of the Artillery watched the attack and remarked,

'The Jack Tars seemed mad for blood, for they charged up the hill in any formation banging away right and left, driving the Zulu before them. The company of 'The Buffs' did their best to

The battlefield memorial at Nyezane which is placed over the graves of the British casualties of the battle.

keep up with the sailors, but were not equal to the occasion, as they had been 'doubled' up from the rear in order to take part in the attack.'

A body of the NNC advanced to their left to support the advance but the Zulu held their ground and the attack stalled A number of the sailors were hit by gunfire. The panting company of Buffs now came up, led by Lieutenant-Colonel Parnell, their commanding officer, and the attack regained momentum. However, about 100 yards from the *umuzi* the attack again ground to a halt as 'The Buffs' began to take casualties. Campbell sent for the remaining half company of sailors and the Royal Marines but before they could come up a final push drove the Zulu from their position. The NNC driving forward in support ejected the last remnants of the force from the burning *umuzi*. Everywhere now the Zulu were in retreat, using Wombane as a shield against the British fire. The high ground was cleared and the bush scoured for any parties of the enemy that might still be lurking. It was an hour and a half since the first shot had been fired. Pearson had been caught in the open but survived a determined Zulu attack. Or at least the attack of the Zulu left had been determined. After the battle there were recriminations among those who had taken part in the battle. The warriors of the uMxhapho who had formed the left horn accused the older men of the uDlambedlu and izinGulube of not pressing their attack on the right. It was reported that Cetshwayo was also angry with Godide for not taking a more active part in the battle.

Pearson was determined to show the Zulu that his advance had not been checked. A burial party dug a large grave for the British casualties. Twelve men had been killed, another twenty wounded of which two would later die. There was no time or inclination to bury the Zulu dead who were spread over a very wide area. Official estimates put them at over 400 with many hundreds more wounded. By midday the column was back on the march as the 130 wagons were dragged painfully slowly up the hill. Pearson advanced a further four miles before ordering camp to be made. It was well after dark before the last of the wagons came in. After the men had eaten, exhausted, they turned in for the night. As Colour-Sergeant Burnett of the 99th wrote, they had had a day of 'terribly earnest work'.

Chapter Four

Eshowe – Besieged

Despite their hard work on 22nd January there was to be no rest for the men of No.1 Column the following day. 'Stand to' was sounded at 3.00am, as a precaution against an early morning attack, and shortly after 5.00am the column was on the march once more. Pearson was determined to move on to Eshowe as quickly as possible to fulfil the initial part of his orders by establishing a major supply depot there, utilizing the deserted mission's buildings. These final five miles were gruelling for both men and beasts as they made the long slow climb up the track to Eshowe. It was about 10.00am when the head of the column rolled in, but another five hours before it was reunited with the tail. Pearson was delighted to find that the buildings on which so much depended were intact. It was a beautiful spot. Well-established orchards, a garden and fine trees surrounded the church, house, schoolroom and store, while a clear stream ran close by. As pleasant as it appeared, for the engineer officer, Captain Wynne, the spot was less than idyllic. As the man responsible for putting the supply depot into a state of defence he considered the position most unfavourable. The area of the mission was commanded by slightly higher ground to the north and south, while to the west a deep ravine approached to within about seventy yards of the church.

Captain Wynne, RE; the architect of the Eshowe defences.

However, the buildings were crucial to the safe storage of the supplies and therefore Wynne had to make the best of a poor position.

The following day Wynne began to trace out an entrenchment to contain all the buildings while the men of the column cleared away the thick bush which grew close up to the mission station. To everyone's sadness, including his own, Wynne decided that the orchards would have to be cut down too.

The heavy physical work of digging out the ditch and piling up the earth inside to form ramparts continued, as did the backbreaking work of clearing the bush. A convoy of empty wagons was formed to collect more supplies and this set out to make the return journey to the Thukela on 25th January, accompanied by four companies of infantry, two companies of the NNC and a few mounted men. As the work continued on 26th January Pearson received a curious letter from Sir Bartle Frere, the High Commissioner, which somewhat vaguely informed him that Durnford, the commander of No.2 Column, was dead and that his black troops had been attacked and defeated. It went on to say that Chelmsford had fought an action too and had been victorious. There was no suggestion as to where these incidents had taken place. The last information Pearson had was that Durnford was on the Thukela at the Middle Drift, covering the Zululand/Natal border. This was worrying news. Did it mean the Zulus had crossed into Natal and could now be threatening his rear? Without any clear information Pearson determined to carry on until he received more details.

The following day work continued as normal at Eshowe while the mounted men rode north to reconnoitre the route by which the column would advance once the entrenchments were complete. It was not until 28th January that Pearson was finally made aware that something had gone terribly wrong. Although sent by Lord Chelmsford, even this note did not tell the whole story:

'Consider all my instructions cancelled and act in whatever manner you think most desirable in the interests of the column under your command. Should you consider the garrison of

The post at Eshowe. This picture clearly shows the mission buildings and the strong entrenchment which surrounded it.

Ekowe [Eshowe] too far advanced to be fed with safety, you can withdraw it.

'Hold however, if possible, the post on the Zulu side of the Lower Thukela. You must be prepared to have the whole Zulu force down upon you. Do away with tents, and let the men take shelter under the wagons, which will then be in position for defence, and hold so many more supplies.'

It was startling news, but what did it mean? Pearson called his officers together to discuss the situation in what became a council of war. Initially the meeting moved towards a retreat but eventually the decision to stay was taken. The full story of what had forced this change of plan, the disaster at Isandlwana, was not received at Eshowe until 2nd February.

Once the decision to stay had been taken, Eshowe became galvanized into a new fury of activity. Pearson recalled the mounted men who had been out on another patrol and ordered their commander, Brevet Major Barrow, to return with his command to the Lower Thukela, along with the men of the NNC. Pearson considered there was neither the space nor foodstuffs to accommodate these men within the fort that was rapidly taking shape. There was no time to waste and Barrow's men, many of whom were members of the Natal Volunteer Corps, were not even given time to collect their personal belongings from the wagons. All tents outside the entrenchments were struck; from now on everyone was to sleep inside the earth walls. The wagons were also driven inside, forming a second line behind the ramparts; the remainder being lined up on an east/west line across the centre of the

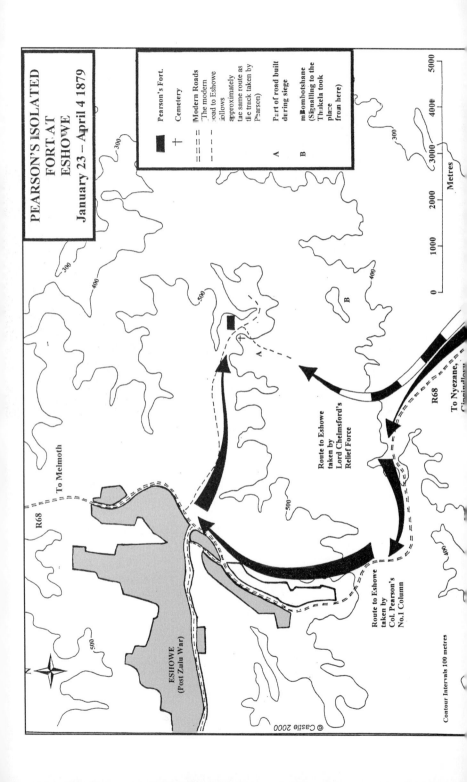

PEARSON'S ISOLATED
FORT AT
ESHOWE
January 23 – April 4 1879

Pearson's Fort.

✝ Cemetery

= = = Modern Roads
- - - The modern
road to Eshowe
follows
approximately
the same route as
the track taken by
Pearson)

A ▪ Part of road built
during siege

B ▪ Mombothshane
(Signalling to the
Thukela took
place
from here)

Metres

0   1000   2000   3000   4000   5000

To Melmoth
R68

ESHOWE
(Post Zulu War)

N

Route to Eshowe
taken by
Lord Chelmsford's
Relief Force

Route to Eshowe
taken by
Col. Pearson's
No.1 Column

R68
To Nyezane,
Gingindlovu

Contour Intervals 100 metres

© Castle 2000

The church inside the fort, photographed at the end of the war; the buildings were ruined by the Zulu after Pearson withdrew.

fort. Such was the concern caused by the news, that even officers were observed wielding pick and shovel in an effort to complete the defences. Before the day was over Pearson's men were boosted by the arrival of a convoy of wagons that had set out from the Lower Thukela on 22nd January. Its safe arrival, along with that of its escort was a great relief to the garrison.

Pearson now took an inventory and initially calculated he had enough food to last the garrison about three weeks, but this was later revised. The mainstay of the garrison was the six companies of 2/3rd Regiment, 'The Buffs', and three companies of the 99th Regiment. These were bolstered by a Naval Brigade, artillery, a few mounted men whose horses had been unfit to return to the border, and representatives of the commissariat, transport and hospital departments as well as a company of the Natal Native Pioneers and forty of the NNC, both black and white. In addition there were numbers of wagon conductors,

The garrison at Eshowe was plagued by sudden alarms; here the Naval Brigade rush to man the ramparts.

drivers, leaders and servants. The total strength of the garrison was 1,799 men, of whom 1461 were considered combat troops. In addition to the rifles of the infantry companies, the garrison could boast a Gatling gun, four 7pdr artillery pieces, two 24pdr rocket tubes and a 9pdr rocket trough.

The nerves of the garrison were always on edge. Each night the peace was broken by a fresh false alarm which forced everyone to man the ramparts and peer into the dark of the African night, straining their eyes for a sight of an enemy that was not there. Although there had yet been no tangible threat to the garrison, nerves were no more relaxed during the day, and when a body of Zulu passed the fort at some distance on 30th January, work was abandoned and the ramparts lined once more. The stress and strain of his responsibilities and the oppressive heat were beginning to tell on Wynne. It was not long

A section of the ditch (north side) surrounding Colonel Pearson's fort at Eshowe. The horses of the garrison were picketed along this line at night.

before the effects of this heat on the cramped garrison, coupled with the torrential rains at night, soon lead to outbreaks of disease. The first man of the garrison to succumb was Private Kingston of 2/3rd who died on 1st February. Pearson recognized he would not be the last and gave orders for a cemetery to be created on the slopes of the ravine to the west of the fort.

That night Pearson considered his position. Groups of Zulu were moving freely in the area and communications with the Thukela were hampered. He had still received no firm details as to what had occurred to Chelmsford's force. The situation was not good and he came to the conclusion that he must consider the fort at Eshowe in a state of siege. Accordingly he issued orders that the garrison would go on to three-quarter rations with immediate effect. The following day he finally received the news of the defeat at Isandlwana. He was now more convinced than ever that it would be a mistake to try and make a dash for the border and abandon the fort. Instead he wrote to Chelmsford asking for reinforcements to be sent to him to bring his battalions up to full strength. This request was rejected on the grounds that the men were needed for the defence of Natal. He wrote again asking for a supply convoy with two companies of Buffs to form part of the escort. In exchange he would send back the three companies of the 99th currently at Eshowe in an attempt to form a more cohesive garrison, with the majority of the fighting men drawn from one battalion as was the normal practice. Chelmsford meanwhile had plans of his own and had written to Pearson stressing that he wanted him to return to the Thukela himself and bring with him part of the garrison. Pearson called another council of war to discuss the situation with his officers. With the spectre of Isandlwana still fresh in everyone's mind, it was generally considered to be a foolish move to chance their luck with a dash to the border. Wynne also pointed out that he felt the perimeter of the entrenchment could not be effectively redrawn so that a reduced garrison could man it. He concluded that a new entrenchment would need to be dug. Having considered the options, all agreed that they could not follow Chelmsford's orders. Pearson sent a note back to the border explaining the situation but added that if Chelmsford was adamant and issued confirming orders he would march. By now though the Zulu operating in the area had closed in and held a loose enveloping cordon around the position. Communication was cut and there could be no confirming reply.

With no other options the men returned to the task of completing the defences. By 9th February the principal works were in place.

The cemetery on the slope of the fort, photographed in 1879.

The cemetery at Eshowe today. Some of the graves post date the Zulu War.

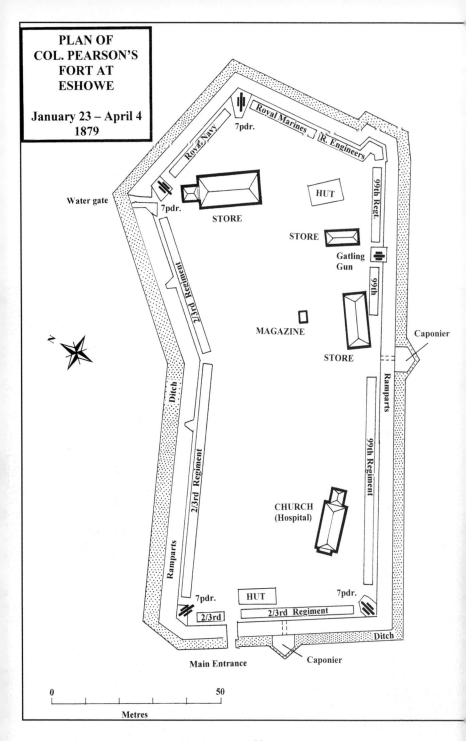

PLAN OF COL. PEARSON'S FORT AT ESHOWE

January 23 – April 4 1879

Royal Navy
Royal Marines
R. Engineers
7pdr.
Water gate
7pdr.
99th Regt.
STORE
HUT
STORE
Gatling Gun
99th
2/3rd Regiment
MAGAZINE
STORE
Caponier
Ditch
Ramparts
2/3rd Regiment
99th Regiment
CHURCH (Hospital)
Ramparts
7pdr.
HUT
7pdr.
2/3rd
2/3rd Regiment
Ditch
Main Entrance
Caponier

0   50
Metres

Wynne and his officers had designed an earthwork that featured many of the latest advancements in the science of fortification. The ditch around the position was sunk to a depth of seven feet (just over two metres) and varied between ten and thirteen feet wide (three and four metres). The ramparts were six feet high (just under two metres) and the main entrance, at the western end, had a drawbridge as did a smaller gate at the north-eastern corner, used by fatigue parties tasked with collecting water from the stream. There were even caponiers in the southern and western ditches that enabled men to remain under cover while firing along the line of the ditches. In addition firing platforms had been constructed for the artillery.

A caponier – a covered way which allowed troops to fire through loopholes down the length of the ditch – suggests the impressive scope of the fortifications.

The substantial defences of the fort at Eshowe must have impressed the watching Zulu as they observed this frantic activity from the comfortable shade of a well-positioned tree. It is a true monument to the skills of Wynne and his fellow Royal Engineers, combined with the energy of the garrison that it is still possible to visit the remains of the fort today. Although they were only constructed from the rich earth of Zululand, the ditches and ramparts of this isolated British outpost still stand defiant. Having continued your drive northwards from Nyezane on the R68 to the outskirts of the modern town of Eshowe there is a crossroads. Take the right turn towards the township of Gezinsila (renamed Prince Dinuzulu suburb in 2000 – both signs are currently in use) and after about one and a half miles you will reach the remains of Pearson's fort. It is situated on the left side of the road and can be located by looking out for the cemetery that marks the western edge of the fort. The cemetery post-dates the 1879 fort and is part of the Norwegian Mission.

At times the area of the fort can become very overgrown but by climbing up onto one of the grassy ramparts it is possible to look out across the whole of the site and let your mind allocate places to 1800 men, their wagons and stores. A stroll along the rampart will take you around the whole perimeter of Pearson's position. It may be a sunny day when you make your visit but spare a thought for the sentries who trudged up and down in the pouring rain on this very spot, all those years ago, nervously peering out into the darkness.

A walk across the central areas of the fort will reveal various grassy humps and bumps. These are the foundations of the church and other buildings; tangible evidence of the very reason why Pearson was drawn to this spot in 1879.

Having sent all his mounted men back to the Thukela, Pearson was lacking in a means to gather information beyond the environs of the fort. To solve this problem Captain Shervinton, NNC, gathered a group of volunteers together, mounted them on officers' horses and on those recovering from sickness and took the field under the name 'The Uhlans'. Early in February one of Shervinton's patrols came under long distance fire and numerous observations of parties of Zulu close to the fort were reported during the day. Later on another patrol observed a large group, 2,000 strong, a couple of miles away. The nerves of the sentries were strained that night and when a movement was detected south-west of the fort after dark, first one shot rang out swiftly followed by several others. The artillery were about to join the

A view of the interior of the fort at Eshowe looking at part of the northern ramparts which were manned by 'The Buffs'. Sadly the fort is more often than not in an overgrown condition these days.

mounting crescendo when the order to cease fire was given as no more movement could be detected. In the morning it was discovered that the 'enemy' had been a shirt and pair of trousers left out overnight to dry on a bush. Shervinton's patrol again came under fire from the same hill as the previous day. Determined to nip this in the bud he led a small group of volunteers up the hill in the early hours of the next morning. As the Zulu approached to take up their positions Shervinton sprung the trap, opened fire, and drove them away. They never occupied the hill again.

Pearson did his best to keep his men occupied. Wire entanglements and pits with sharpened stakes, designed to break up any Zulu attacks, were added to the defences. Men were required to act as cattle guards and piquets formed a cordon around the fort to warn of enemy movement. But disease was gaining a stronger hold and the church, which had been converted into a hospital, was soon crammed with patients.

Gradually Pearson's confidence began to return. The Zulu had failed to attack him when he was at his most vulnerable. Now the fort was complete and would, he felt, be able to withstand anything the enemy could throw at him. On 19th February he rode out on a reconnaissance patrol while a foraging party was sent out for the first time to raid Zulu gardens, returning with supplies of mealies and pumpkins. These raids became regular occurrences and helped to boost the dwindling food supplies of the garrison. Three days later, while the cattle were being herded out to their grazing ground, their drivers came under attack from Zulu fire. Two companies of 2/3rd were ordered out and with a few Uhlans were successful in driving them off. After this incident the cattle were accompanied by a large infantry guard each day. The raids continued and the variety of produce they added to the garrison's monotonous diet was much appreciated. Indeed, on 23rd February, Pearson agreed to add further to this by holding an auction of foodstuffs that had been discovered in the personal baggage of the Natal Volunteers who had been sent back to the Thukela at the end of January. Tins of sardines, salmon, pots of jam, bottles of Worcester sauce and even a 12lb ham were sold for extraordinary prices and gleefully consumed by the successful bidders. However the hospital was still full with many patients in a serious condition and by the end of February seven of the garrison were lying in the cemetery on the slopes of the ravine.

The cemetery is just a short distance from the site of Pearson's fort. As you leave the site turn to the left along the road and in a short distance a track turns off to the right. This is the start of the actual road built by Pearson's men in 1879. Just a few yards along the bush opens out and the ground falls away on the right hand side into the ravine that had caused Captain Wynne concern when he first arrived. Lying before you in terraced rows are the mixture of stone monuments and metal crosses that mark the last resting place of those who died of disease far from home while defending the fort at Eshowe. They are still at their posts to this day.

Although Pearson and his men had daily expected to see a vast Zulu army descend on their position this was completely at odds with the Zulu strategy. The senior commander in the coastal area was the king's brother, Prince Dabulamanzi kaMpande. It was he who had led the unsuccessful attack, contrary to orders, against Rorke's Drift in January. This time there was to be no costly repeat by attacking another fortified position. Cetshwayo was angry that the British had set up camp deep within his country but needed to draw them out into the open before he could launch an attack. To this end about 500 men surrounded Eshowe each day with orders to goad and irritate the British in an attempt to force them to move out and attack. Behind this front line some 5,000 warriors were based on local military and civilian homesteads, awaiting the order to attack. The attacks on British patrols and harassment of cattle guards were all part of this strategy. British officers accompanying patrols that encountered these frontline warriors reported how the Zulu would shout insults, threats and warnings at them as they passed. Lieutenant Lloyd, RA., heard one warrior cry out, 'Come out of that hole you old women; we always thought the English would fight, and not burrow under the ground!' Lloyd's acquaintance went on to say that he hoped to come and share his excellent coffee and sugar soon. Another officer reported a similar exchange, 'Why don't you take more care of Cetshwayo's cattle and get them fatter? He will want them soon.' It was not until 1st March that Pearson was tempted to leave the security of the fort in strength and go over to the offensive.

A recent patrol had located the site of one of the main *ikhanda* in the area, about seven miles to the north-east of Eshowe. A couple of miles beyond that they had also discovered one of Dabulamanzi's personal homesteads. Having been unable to strike a significant blow against the Zulu since the action at Nyezane, Pearson decided that a

The south-east corner of the fort. The Royal Engineers, who built a stockade of timber and sandbags at this point to allow two levels of firing, manned this section.

successful raid in force against these two enemy rallying points would be a great boon to the morale of the garrison. It could also serve to force the encircling cordon onto the back foot. At 2.00am on the morning of 1st March Pearson marched out with a mixed force about 500 strong, drawn from the 2/3rd Regiment , 99th Regiment, Royal Marines, Royal Artillery, Royal Engineers, the Uhlans and Natal Native Pioneers. In a later account Lieutenant Lloyd, RA., described the march:

'The night was luckily clear, for we struck a path straight across country, under the guidance of one of our Zulu allies. It was the most silent march I ever took part in, and will be long remembered. All orders were given in whispers, we seemed to glide along, and yet the gun-wheels creaked outrageously, or one seemed to imagine so.'

The head of the column came into sight of the military homestead, eSiqwakeni, just as dawn was breaking. It was clear that the occupants were all asleep in their huts and surprise was on Pearson's side. However, the opportunity was wasted. Rather than send his infantry and mounted men in, Pearson preferred to wait another ten minutes while the artillery 7pdr was brought up. Lieutenant Lloyd continues his story:

'About 500 yards, on a hill to our left, I noticed in the dim light some kraals, and perceived a Zulu strolling leisurely out of one of them. For a few seconds he had his back to us, but quickly turning around no doubt espied our little force wending its way along below. He fled like a hare. The circumstance was at once reported to Col. Pearson, who sent four mounted men to try and cut him off. It was, however, too late, and I feel sure that man upset our plans, for on arriving in sight of the military kraal some few minutes after, we saw to our disgust the whole Zulu impi streaming out of it with all their goods and chattels in their arms.'

Pearson ordered the Engineers forward to clear the ground to the flanks of his proposed line of advance but it was all too late. The main body of the column never got into action. A party of mounted men rode into the abandoned homestead and put it to the torch. The 7pdr lobbed two or three rounds into the fleeing Zulu but an attempt to capture a prisoner for interrogation failed when those appointed to the task came under a heavy fire. Recalling these men Pearson decided he could achieve little else, turned the column and began his march back to Eshowe. Realizing they had little to fear those warriors who had fled now also turned and began to fire on the rearguard and flanks of the column as it retired. The Zulu kept up their attacks most of the way back to the fort. Using the bush well, they would appear, fire, then melt away again before appearing at the next suitable piece of ground. This was the second occasion on which Pearson's men had witnessed Zulu tactics at first hand and again they were impressed with what they saw. Lloyd in concluding his account wrote:

'It was really a pleasure to watch the manner in which these Zulu skirmished. No crowding, no delay, as soon as they were driven from one cover they would hasten rapidly to the next awkward bit of country through which our column would have to pass. Luckily for us their shooting was inferior, or we should have suffered severely.'

Everyone returned safely from the morning's adventure but there was a feeling among some of the officers that it had not been a well-run affair. However, there was no time to dwell on the matter. The following day there was something new to occupy the garrison as a fever of excitement swept through the fort. A mounted man patrolling southwards noticed a flickering light far off in the direction of the Thukela. A group of officers came out to investigate and pondered a number of theories as to its origin until it suddenly dawned on them – it was a signal; an attempt at communication by sun flashes. A transport officer, Captain Pelly Clarke, was caught up in the excitement. In his account he exclaimed,

'Great was our joy! Faces that had for long borne an anxious and desponding look, assumed a more hopeful aspect; new energy, new life, seemed to be instilled in us, as we found all was not over.'

Late the following morning the flashes were observed again. The flashes were spelling out letters of the Morse code and bit by bit they were turned into a message, but it was a slow process as there was much cloud. It was only on the fourth day, 6th March, that the full message could be read. Pearson was informed that a relief column, over 1,000 men strong, would be setting out from the Thukela on 13th March. The indefatigable Captain Wynne concentrated on trying to construct a means by which to reply to the message, as no signalling equipment had been issued to any of Chelmsford's columns at the beginning of the war. Although heliographs were part of British Army equipment, there were none in southern Africa at this time. Wynne tried a hot air balloon made from tracing paper and powered by a paraffin burner and a large pivoting black screen of tarpaulin, but both failed to achieve the required result. Other officers found a large mirror packed away in the baggage and began to experiment with that. A length of pipe from the church was pressed into service to help aim the flashes but that did not work either. Wynne made another pivoting screen but although he brought it into operation it could not be seen at the river. Finally, on 14th March, Captain Beddoes of the Natal Native Pioneers perfected a system using the mirror, a barrel and wire aiming rods. After fifty-one days of isolation two-way communication had been opened.

With news that a relief party would soon be on the way, Pearson turned his attention to creating a new road to the fort that would shorten the distance the column would have to march. The work began in earnest but very heavy rains initially thwarted it. When work was possible the Zulu cordon closed in and opened a harassing fire. The Zulu were indeed becoming more daring. On 7th March Corporal Carson of the 99th Regiment, attached to the Mounted Infantry, was ambushed while out on vedette duty. About twelve or fifteen Zulu leapt at his horse. A spear sank into the horse's rump as it galloped away, while a ragged volley followed Carson and his mount. He was shot through both thighs by one bullet as another struck his hand leaving two fingers attached only by a sliver of skin. A third bullet smashed into the lock of his carbine that was slung across his back. Carson made it safely back to the fort where he was fortunate to make a full recovery, minus his two fingers.

Work on the new road continued but Wynne was becoming

Corporal Carson, 99th Regiment, ambushed by Zulu fights for his life and escapes bearing a number of wounds. S. Bourquin

Some of the buildings inside the fort, photographed at the end of the war; they were ruined by the Zulu after Pearson withdrew.

frustrated with its slow progress. The Zulu attacks were demanding the attention of more and more of the men, leaving few to actually carry out the required work. Each day when the work parties withdrew, their elusive opponents would come forward and disrupt what progress had been made. To prevent any recurrence of this a booby trap was devised and left in the roadway. When next the Zulu advanced, an unsuspecting warrior pulled a stake from the ground exploding a landmine made from dynamite. This appeared to have the desired effect for after this incident the roadworks were left unmolested.

Over 11th and 12th March large numbers of warriors were seen moving southwards. It was clear to the garrison that the Zulu intelligence system was working well and they knew a relief column was about to set out from the border. The road was finished for the 13th March but Wynne, who had been in poor health, reported sick and never returned to work. That morning excitement was high as Pearson ordered a party of about 600 men to be ready to march out to meet the relief force that was due to start from the Thukela. Then followed a crushing blow to the morale of the garrison. A message flickered in the distance. The relief was to be postponed until 1st April.

An air of melancholy settled over the garrison of Eshowe. Not only were they going to have to suffer almost another three weeks of isolation, but the monotony of the diet took a turn for the worse when the last of the slaughter oxen was consumed. From now on the meat ration would be drawn from the almost inedible trek oxen. Heavy rains returned; disease continued to claim victims and the Zulu cordon was still tight, leading to a fatal attack on Private Kent while on vedette duty on 17th March. In his journal, which he kept throughout the siege, Gunner Carroll of the Royal Marine Artillery explained the feelings of the garrison:

'Having had very buoyant hopes of soon being relieved for the past week or so, this news of a further delay rather damped our spirits. Our situation is very miserable, not enough to eat, the 8 ounces of biscuit we get daily being maggoty and mouldy. The mealy meal we get (4 ounces) we make porridge of. No vegetables. We have been exposed to all weathers for the past seven or eight weeks having had no tents pitched during that time, sleeping under wagons at night, with a wagon cover to protect us from the rain, often having to sit up all night holding it. When raining hard sometimes being completely washed out. We wear our accoutrements, with seventy rounds of ammunition in them, night and day, being severely punished if anyone is found with them off at night.

'The health of the troops is very bad, nearly half are sick – the number of little mounds, fenced around with the staves of barrels, and bearing a rude wooden cross at the head on which is cut a simple inscription are becoming more numerous everyday.'

Thankfully for the garrison it was not long before these low spirits were lifted once more. On 19th March a brave black runner forced his way through from the Thukela and handed Pearson news that the relief force was to begin its advance on 29th March. Reanimated, Pearson ordered a raid to be made the following day, while in the fort the wagons that had become part of the defences were extricated and repairs carried out in preparation for the march back.

On 30th March the sight the garrison had waited so long to see could be observed through telescopes. Chelmsford's relief column was approaching the amaTigulu river about thirteen miles distant. Most of the following day they spent crossing the river, but mounted men were seen scouting ahead and spirits continued to soar. As darkness fell on the night of 1st April Pearson's men watched the twinkling lights of Chelmsford's laager. Eventually they turned in for the night, eagerly anticipating what the morning would bring.

Chapter Five

GINGINDLOVU – BRAVERY AGAINST BULLETS

For Lord Chelmsford the weeks after the disaster at Isandlwana had been a difficult time. His invasion plans lay in ruins. The centre column had been thrown out of Zululand, Pearson's column was isolated and surrounded deep in enemy country and only Wood's No.4 Column still had any freedom of movement. The war had started without the sanction of the home government and now Chelmsford was forced to report a major setback so soon after the campaign had begun. What is more, if Cetshwayo now chose to move over to the offensive Chelmsford had little to offer in defence of Natal. Luckily for him and the colonists of Natal, Cetshwayo had no intention of pushing his advantage in this way. Although his warriors had produced an overwhelming victory at Isandlwana they had returned home shocked by the severity of the fighting and the casualties they had sustained. After the battle the majority of fighting men returned to their homes where they underwent the traditional post-battle rituals to cleanse themselves of spiritual contamination and were not available to carry the war into Natal. Besides, Cetshwayo had not wanted the war; it had been forced upon him and he naively hoped that now the British had suffered defeat they might be prepared to discuss peace. For the British this was out of the question. A defeat such as Isandlwana had to be avenged, there could be no question of leaving such business unfinished.

Before he could return to the offensive Chelmsford needed to rebuild his army. While the British nation was stunned by the news, the home government had been swift to respond to the news of Isandlwana. Within a day the War Office had sent out orders informing two cavalry regiments, six infantry battalions, two artillery batteries, along with detachments of engineers, service corps and hospital corps, to bring themselves up to strength for war. Other reinforcements were drawn in from outposts of the Empire. The garrison of St. Helena, a company of the 88th Regiment and an artillery battery, were embarked on HMS *Shah* as soon as the news was received. They were landed at Durban on 6th March with a naval contingent 400 strong, drawn from the ship's company. The 57th Regiment, one of the battalions authorized by the War Office, landed from Ceylon on 11th March and another company of the 88th soon followed from Mauritius. The first of the reinforcements from Britain was the 91st Regiment, landed at Durban on 17th March. They were followed three days later by six companies of the 3/60th Rifles. It was these two battalions, along with the 57th Regiment and the five companies of the 99th who had not been incarcerated at Eshowe, that were to form the backbone of the force detailed to the relief of Pearson's isolated command.

The weeks following Isandlwana dragged on for those positioned at the Lower Drift. In fact there was probably even less to occupy these men than for those at Eshowe. The defences of Fort Tenedos, an entrenchment built on the Zulu bank of the river, were strengthened but there was no demonstration of aggressive intentions by the Zulu in the area. Until reinforcements arrived there was little that could be achieved. As highlighted in the previous chapter, Chelmsford had hoped to lead a relief force to Eshowe during February, one which required Pearson to march out and meet it halfway. Pearson had been reluctant to commit his men to this enterprise and when communications were cut the plan was abandoned. It is perhaps lucky for all concerned that it was, as Chelmsford had only seven companies of regulars, Barrow's mounted men and a number of naval personnel for the task. Sir Bartle Frere was rather surprised when he was made aware of Chelmsford's aborted plan. In response he wrote,

'... I was also very glad to hear you had given up the idea of going towards Ekowe [Eshowe] but, till I heard you had

The area around the Lower Drift of the Thukela. Fort Tenedos is in the foreground while on the skyline, left, is Fort Pearson. The group of trees on the right skyline marks the site of the cemetery on page 59.

abandoned it, I had no idea you thought of anything so rash. It would never do to have YOU shut up, or even out of daily post range.'

There was little anyone could do but wait.

The inability to communicate had been just as great a source of frustration to those at the Lower Thukela as it had been for the garrison of Eshowe. That first flickering signal witnessed by the beleaguered garrison on 2nd March, which had been observed with such joy, had been produced by a bedroom mirror 'borrowed' from a nearby hotel. It was to be May before any heliographs were available to Chelmsford's army.

While the inactivity continued, Lord Chelmsford's manpower gradually increased. The 2nd Regiment of the NNC, which had been sent back from Eshowe to the border in January, had been dismissed to their homes. Now they were ordered to return to duty and reorganized. The old regimental system was dropped and in its place the two battalions were reformed as the 4th and 5th battalions NNC. To strengthen the morale of the men all were now issued with firearms, although for many this still meant outdated percussion weapons. John Dunn provided another useful addition to the force. Dunn had begun hunting professionally in Zululand in 1847 when only seventeen years old. Now, thirty years later, he had gained wealth and power from his trading activities and his role as advisor to Cetshwayo. He had been invited to settle in Zululand and given control of a large extent of land north of the Lower Thukela Drift where he built two homesteads and

adopted the Zulu lifestyle. When war threatened he had withdrawn into Natal with about 2,000 of his adherents hoping to remain neutral, but now increased pressure from Chelmsford saw Dunn join the reforming army, bringing with him about 150 of his trained hunters who acted as scouts.

Despite this progress it was to be the second half of March before the force designated to march to the relief of Eshowe gathered strength. On 13th March the naval contingent from HMS *Shah* arrived, followed by the first of the regular reinforcements, the 57th Regiment, who made camp on 22nd March. Over the next few days the 91st, 3/60th and another naval contingent, 200 strong from HMS *Boadicea*, joined them. Chelmsford rode into camp on 23rd March and it was clear to everyone that it would not be long before the march commenced.

Now the initial shock of Isandlwana had worn off at home Chelmsford was becoming the target for increasing criticism for the defeat. Determined to avoid any repeat, he formulated strict orders for the management of the relief column while on the march and for the security of the camp at night. On 25th March Chelmsford issued

Gatling gun crew from HMS *Boadicea*.

instructions for the first of the relief force to be ferried across the Thukela. The entire process took four days to complete. Then, at dawn on the morning of 29th March, the signal was given and the column set out on the long-awaited mission to relieve the besieged garrison of Eshowe.

Chelmsford now had command of a force of 5,500 fighting men which he formed into two brigades. The 1st Brigade, under the command of Lieutenant-Colonel Law, RA., was formed of the 91st, five companies of the 99th, two companies of 2/3rd and the naval contingents of *Shah* and *Tenedos*, with two 9-pdr guns, two 24-pdr rocket tubes and a Gatling gun. They were supported by the Mounted Infantry, Natal Volunteer Guides, Jantje's Native Horse, the 5th Battalion NNC and Dunn's Scouts. The 2nd Brigade was commanded by Lieutenant Colonel Pemberton, 3/60th, its infantry component being formed by the 57th, 3/60th and the naval contingent from *Boadicea* with a Gatling gun and another two 24-pdr rocket tubes. With them marched the 4th Battalion NNC, No.2 Troop Natal Horse and Mafunzi's Mounted Natives. However, this was not to be a fast-moving flying column. Attached to it and dramatically slowing progress were forty-four carts and ninety-four wagons. Crammed into these were ten days' supplies for the relief force and a month's provisions for the new garrison that Chelmsford planned to install at Eshowe.

The first part of the march was across familiar ground as it followed the path to St. Andrew's mission, from where the signallers at the Lower Thukela had opened communications with Eshowe. From there the column was directed on a route further to the east of the one taken by Pearson on his advance. Here was evidence of Chelmsford's more cautious approach. This new route avoided the potentially dangerous areas of bush through which Pearson had moved and followed a route through more open grasslands. The recent heavy rains had ensured that the ground was soaked and slowed progress considerably. Lieutenant Backhouse of the 2/3rd kept a regular diary throughout the war and recorded some of the difficulties of the day:

> 'Got nothing to eat until 2.00pm except some bread and coffee before we started... Marched about 10 miles, many men fell out as we carry greatcoats, and they were soaking wet... slept under a wagon with the rest of our fellows: we all got a tot of rum, evening, to keep out the cold.'

By the end of the first day the column had reached the Nyoni river where they made camp for the night. In accordance with Chelmsford's

Lord Chelmsford's relief column on the march to Eshowe.

new regulations the first task now was to form laager. A staff officer,
Captain Molyneux, recorded the confusion.

> '...that night the wagon drivers , who had had no practice in
> laagering, got so out of hand that the laager was made anyhow,
> and it would only hold one third of our oxen. So much for our
> first laager on our first trek.'

Guy Dawney, a civilian adventurer, who had come out from England
to see some action had used his influence to get an attachment to the
5th Battalion, NNC. He arrived at camp after dark and described it as,

> '...a mass of confusion – native contingent, Gough and
> Davis's battalion [5th] outside the shelter trench, wagons drawn
> up inside that, and the interior a jumble of carts, kicking horses,
> mules, oxen, men &c. &c.'

Chelmsford had insisted that no tents should be brought along so those
who were unable to secure a berth under a wagon slept out under their

sodden greatcoats. Heavy rain returned. Before he settled down for the night Lieutenant Backhouse added to his diary, 'The General has come in command, I hope we shall not make a mess of it this time.'

Due to the rain of the previous night, the start was delayed until about 7.00am on the second day. The first obstacle to be dealt with was the Nyoni river. The wagons were forced to cross one at a time and it soon became necessary to cut down branches to place in the river to prevent them becoming stuck. Much to the happiness of those who had been soaked to the skin during the night, the day was warm and sunny and everyone's clothes dried out. Food, however, still seems to have been a problem. Lieutenant Backhouse complained,

'Our commissariat arrangements don't seem too good as we get nothing before we start in the morning and one has to smoke to keep down the hunger.'

The newly arrived Dawney also felt aggrieved, 'Got some food about 5, till then eating raw Kafir corn.'

Having dragged all the wagons and carts across the river, the column moved on about eight miles and made camp on the south bank of the next river, the amaTigulu. Work immediately commenced in constructing the laager. The wagons were drawn up in a rough square and a trench dug all the way around. The earth from the trench was piled up so as to form a rampart. The oxen were driven inside the laager while the men were allocated spaces between the wagons and ramparts. Molyneux detected an improvement and wrote, 'this was better than the previous day's work... the laager this time was large enough and fairly well made.' That evening the rain returned causing the river to rise dramatically.

As the men of the column shook off the stiffness of another cold and wet night, it became clear that the crossing of the river would be a major exercise. The night's rain had widened it to about forty yards and raised it to a depth of four feet. Some of the mounted men and Dunn's Scouts were pushed across the river first, then as they checked the area for any Zulu presence, the 1st Brigade began to cross. The water reached up to the men's armpits in some places but generally it was waist-deep. In order to keep their rifles and ammunition dry they were forced to carry them on their heads. Double spans of oxen, thirty-two beasts strong, were needed to drag each wagon through. It took six hours to get them all across. Because of the great exertion required in forcing the passage of the river, the column made camp for the night less than two miles further on. For the first time since the march had begun small groups of Zulu had been observed during the day but these had melted away when approached. Barrow had led a group of mounted men on a patrol towards the Mlalazi river, destroying a large deserted homestead that belonged to a half-brother of the king. It was this operation that the garrison of Eshowe had observed and which was referred to in the previous chapter.

The following day, 1st April, the column formed up and moved off

The amaTigulu drift. Although this photograph was probably taken later, during the second invasion, it gives a clear idea of the difficulties involved in moving an entire column's transport through one narrow river crossing.

at about 7.00am. The countryside now began to change, becoming less open with more areas of bush and trees restricting the view and slowing the march. Occasional halts were called while companies of infantry were sent ahead to sweep through particularly threatening areas to prevent ambush but the only Zulu observed were some way off and in small numbers. A site for the laager was selected, crowning a rise in the ground about a mile south of the Nyezane river, downstream from where Pearson had won his battle on 22nd January and close to the deserted kwaGingindlovu military homestead his men had destroyed the previous day.

Each day the laagering arrangements had been fine-tuned until it had been determined that the wagons should be parked so as to form a square with each side measuring 130 yards. Outside the wagons a ditch was dug at a distance of fifteen yards, the earth forming a rampart about thirty inches high. Molyneux was happy with the position; he wrote that,

'...it was only slightly commanded on the south side, with regular glacis-like slopes on the three others...the laager was finished and the shelter trench marked out in no time. The distances worked out beautifully; we had guns, rockets, or gatlings, at the angles of the trench; an opening in the middle of each face to let the horses and cattle in and out, with four wagons ready to run in and close it at any moment.'

While the laager was being completed Molyneux went out on a reconnaissance with John Dunn. They observed a lot of Zulu activity and it seemed clear that a battle was imminent. Having reported their findings to Chelmsford, Molyneux was struck with how the state of the laager had deteriorated in the two or three hours he had been away. Much to his disgust he found that,

'...the trench was completed but full of water in places, and the state of the ground inside it defies description. When 5,000 human beings, 2,000 oxen and 300 horses have been churning up five acres of very sodden ground... it makes a compost that is neither pretty to look at, easy to move about in, nor nice to smell.'

At the end of another long day a thunderstorm broke over the laager, making the conditions within its confines even worse, and a false alarm forced everyone to stand-to in the rain for an hour. In the distance several Zulu campfires were observed. Lieutenant Backhouse was still confiding to his diary and at the end of the day he penned his frustration, 'We'll make Cetewayo [Cetshwayo] pay for all this discomfort when we get hold of him.'

The progress of this vast, ungainly column as it had been slowly, inexorably closing on Eshowe was well known to Cetshwayo. His well-informed intelligence system had advised him of the build-up of men on the Lower Thukela. He was also painfully aware of the activities of Wood's column in the northwest of his kingdom. By mid March the army had been ordered to reassemble at oNdini after its period of recuperation following Isandlwana. Having carefully considered his options Cetshwayo ordered the main army to oppose Wood, while diverting a smaller force to bolster those currently watching Pearson at Eshowe. With the possibility that the British were going to attempt to send a new force to Eshowe, the opportunity would present itself for a Zulu army to hit it in the open. Reluctant to attack the fortifications at Eshowe, this was just the chance they had been waiting for. Command of the force, which was to absorb a great number of local elements of the regiments that were on their way to fight at Khambula, was given to one of Cetshwayo's trusted friends and advisors, Somopho kaZikhale. This force had begun to gather on 29th March, the day Chelmsford commenced his advance, but it was not until now, the night of 1st/2nd April that all were assembled on the hills north and west of the Nyezane river. Before dawn, and under the cover of a thick mist, the men stirred their chilled bones and moved off silently towards the laager, forming their traditional chest and horns battle formation as they moved.

At dawn, just after 5.00am, a party of mounted black irregulars and Dunn's Scouts moved out from the laager to scour the vicinity for any signs of Zulu activity. Infantry and NNC piquets were still out waiting to be relieved. Chelmsford had announced that there would be no forward movement on this day so the troops would have a chance to rest and recover their strength after their hard work of the last four days. The difficulties of the march had also persuaded Chelmsford to abandon his plans to install a new garrison at Eshowe; the fort was to be abandoned.

Shortly before 6.00am a few odd shots were heard from the direction of the river valley. Those on the north side of the laager tried to ascertain the cause and were greeted by the sight of scouts and piquets rapidly falling back. Beyond them and rapidly approaching the river were two large Zulu columns; away to the west another was observed and then a fourth was seen approaching from the northeast. Estimates suggest that some 11 to 12,000 warriors were converging on the laager. The alarm was sounded, the men fell into their allotted

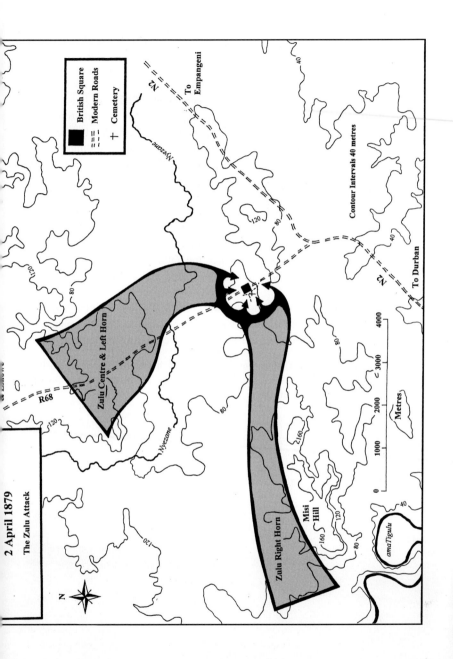

2 April 1879
The Zulu Attack

British Square
Modern Roads
Cemetery

To Empangeni

N2

Contour Intervals 40 metres

Nyezane

To Durban

N2

Zulu Centre & Left Horn

R68

Nyezane

Zulu Right Horn

Misi Hill

amaTigulu

Metres

0   1000   2000   3000   4000

N

positions and the order was given for company volleys to open at 300 yards. There was to be no independent firing. The 3/60th held the centre of the front, or north face, of the laager. The front left corner was secured by a party of Royal Marines and sailors, with two rocket tubes, from HMS *Boadicea* while the front right corner was held by marines from *Shah* and *Tenedos* as well as another group of sailors from *Boadicea*. Their position being strengthened by the addition of a Gatling gun. The right face of the laager was defended by the 57th, sailors from *Shah* with a Gatling and two rocket tubes holding the right rear corner. Two companies of 2/3rd and five companies of the 99th held the left face, with the left rear corner secured by more of *Shah's* sailors with two 9-pdr artillery pieces. The 91st Regiment defended the rear face. The mounted men were distributed between the infantry and wagons on the front and right faces, while the two battalions of NNC were positioned towards the left rear of the laager.

As the men watched in silence the Zulu attack moved on rapidly. Lieutenant Hutton, 3/60th, was fascinated and admired the way they came on:

> 'The Zulu continued to advance, still at a run, until they were about 800 yards from us, when they began to open fire. In spite of the excitement of the moment, we could not but admire the

The battlefield of Gingindlovu, looking north roughly from the position held by the 3/60th Rifles. The main Zulu army had bivouacked in the hills in the left distance on the night before the battle.

Looking west from the position of the square at Gingindlovu towards Misi hill. The Zulu right horn first appeared in this direction.

perfect manner in which these Zulu skirmished. A small knot of five or six would rise and dart through the long grass, dodging from side to side with heads down, rifles and shields kept low and out of sight. They would then suddenly sink into the long grass, and nothing but puffs of curling smoke would show their whereabouts.'

At 800 yards range the crew from the *Boadicea* operating the Gatling on the front right corner asked for permission to check the range. Moments later the tut, tut, tut of the gun burst forth and a swathe was cut through the advancing Zulu. Undaunted, the Zulu continued to advance, taking advantage of the long grass and bush to close with the laager. As they approached to within 400 yards the order was given for the infantry to open fire. It was barely ten minutes since the Zulu had first come into view. The volley that burst forth was remembered by all who heard it. One wrote, 'the whole front of our camp broke into a sheet of flame which ran from corner to corner without intermission.' Yet at that range the effect was limited as the only target was, 'darting figures at irregular intervals and distances.' The Zulu continued to advance into this storm but took advantage of every type of cover, many working their way forwards on their stomachs to avoid the worst of the hail of lead, but still grasping any opportunity to return the fire. However, the movements of men and oxen the previous day in laying out the laager had flattened the grass for about 100 yards all around the position. At this point the Zulu were forced into the open; grasping

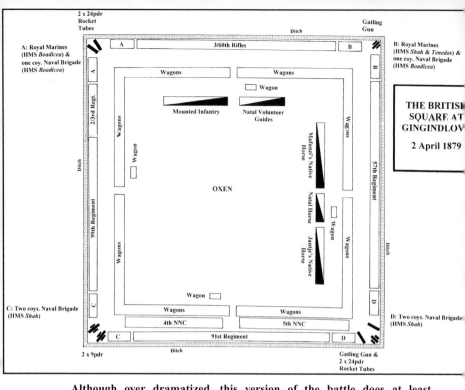

A: Royal Marines (HMS *Boadicea*) & one coy. Naval Brigade (HMS *Boadicea*)

B: Royal Marines (HMS *Shah* & *Tenedos*) & one coy. Naval Brigade (HMS *Boadicea*)

C: Two coys. Naval Brigade (HMS *Shah*)

D: Two coys. Naval Brigade (HMS *Shah*)

2 x 24pdr Rocket Tubes

Gatling Gun

Ditch

3/60th Rifles

Wagons

Wagons

Wagon

Mounted Infantry

Natal Volunteer Guides

2/3rd Regt.

99th Regiment

57th Regiment

Ditch

Ditch

Wagons

Wagons

Wagon

Wagon

Wagons

Wagons

Wagons

OXEN

Mafunzi's Native Horse

Natal Horse

Jantje's Native Horse

Wagon

Wagons

Wagons

4th NNC

5th NNC

Wagon

91st Regiment

2 x 9pdr

Ditch

Gatling Gun & 2 x 24pdr Rocket Tubes

Although over dramatized, this version of the battle does at least accurately depict the British rampart at Gingindlovu. S. Bourquin

their shields and spears they launched themselves at the line held by the 3/60th. The effort on both sides was desperate but the density of fire forced the line of the Zulu attack to veer to its right and seek an easier opening down the left side of the laager. Now the fire of the companies of 'The Buffs' and 99th Regiment was added to the mayhem. Yet the frontal attack had been closer to success than the Zulu realized. After the battle piles of dead were calculated to be lying just 20 to 30 yards from the ditch surrounding the laager but the men who had inflicted these casualties had been anything but steady. A number of observers commented on the performance of the 3/60th, which contained a high percentage of young inexperienced soldiers, products of the new short-service system. One of their own junior officers, 2nd Lieutenant Mynors, was openly frank when he wrote, 'Our men were awfully frightened and nervous at first, could not even speak and shivered from funk.' Others wrote of their fear that the line was about to break. Lieutenant-Colonel Northey, of the regiment, was wounded and taken off to the ambulance but his officers exerted their influence over the men and the crisis passed. Northey died four days later.

In the meantime an attack had developed against the front right corner of the laager from where the Gatling of HMS *Boadicea* was still spitting out destruction. Using the cover of a donga, groups of Zulu had gathered out of the fire before throwing themselves towards the right of the British front line and the Gatling gun. Despite Herculean efforts they could not penetrate the line nor stand in its fire and were forced back to the cover of the donga or the long grass.

The attack that had rolled around to the left face of the laager was met again by a withering fire, this time by the men of 2/3rd and 99th who had fought at Nyezane. Lieutenant Backhouse was with his men, who were drawn up four deep, and awaited the attack as:

'...the guns and rockets opened fire on them, but on they came very pluckily to within 50 yds of us at some places, in spite of the tremendous fire we kept up. I am afraid a good deal of ammunition was wasted as the men could not be stopped from blazing away.'

Although fire discipline had broken down there was no way through for the Zulu. The battle had only been running for about fifteen minutes but the impetus of the chest had been broken. Meanwhile the attack of the right horn, which was sweeping in from the west, was gaining momentum and their bullets were whizzing up the line of the 91st Regiment who were manning the rear face. The advance developed in a similar fashion to that of the chest. Guy Dawney stood

107

Inside the square at the height of the battle.

behind the 91st and observed the attack evolve:

'We could see large bodies moving around behind the first ridges, and the rockets and shells were tried at them; I can't say, though, I was impressed by the accuracy of either... The big bodies of Zulu broke up into skirmishing order before crossing the ridge, and the way they then came on was magnificent. We

kept up a heavy fire at every black figure we saw, but they crawled through the grass, and dodged behind bushes, shooting at us all the time, and soon every bush in front of us held and hid two or three Zulu, and the puffs of smoke showed us they were there.'

It would appear that the fire of the 91st was as devastating as that of the other regiments for Dawney reported that 'no Zulu got nearer to the shelter trench than thirty-one yards.' Unable to break through, the Zulu attack rolled around to the right face of the laager which had been comparatively quiet up to now. Taking advantage of a slope in the ground about 200 yards from the laager, the Zulu were able to concentrate free from the raking fire pouring forth from the 57th Regiment. In fact the sudden appearance of the Zulu on this flank had caused the recall of Major Barrow who had been sent out of the north face with the Mounted Infantry and Volunteers to drive away the Zulu who had fallen back to the long grass on that front. The Zulu advanced bravely once more, into the murderous fire of the 57th, whose well-controlled volleys rang out 'as clear as if they were at Aldershot', but it was now an impossible task and this attack too went to ground.

It was just after 7.00am when Chelmsford sensed that the Zulu attack was spent and gave the order for Barrow to move out across the right face of the laager and attack the Zulu right flank. Leading a half squadron of the Mounted Infantry, Barrow moved out into the open, forcing those Zulu still holding on before the right face to fall back on their comrades in front of the rear face of the laager. The Natal Horse and the two troops of black irregulars now joined Barrow. The Natal Horse opened fire into the Zulu flank and that seemed to be the final straw for the Zulu who began to break. At this point Chelmsford ordered the NNC to advance over the ditch on the rear face and push the Zulu away in conjunction with Barrow. To a trained cavalryman like Barrow this was the moment he had been waiting for and he launched the half squadron of Mounted Infantry into the flank of the retiring Zulu. In his report he recorded that his men,

> '...drew swords and charged the Zulu, who were in large numbers, but utterly demoralized. The actual number killed with the sword was probably few, but the moral effect on the retreating Zulu as the swordsmen closed in on them was very great.'

He was right. The ruthless combined pursuit of mounted men and the NNC swiftly turned retreat into flight. About ninety minutes after it had started the Battle of Gingindlovu was over. In the space of four days the Zulu army had suffered two crushing defeats, here and at Khambula in the north.

The site of the Battle of Gingindlovu is probably the least visual of all the Anglo-Zulu War sites. It is located in the rolling coastal hills in an area which is now dominated by the sugar cane industry. Indeed the site of the laager is now crowned with suger cane and dissected by the

Mounted Infantry pursuing the retreating Zulus. The pursuit at Gingindluvu was particularly savage and many wounded and exhausted warriors were killed as they struggled to cross the Nyezane.

The remains of Zulu dead littering the bare slopes at Gingindlovu a few months after the battle.   S. Bourquin

Brevet Lieutenant-Colonel Northey, mortally wounded at Gingindlovu.

The British dead were buried just outside the laager ramparts.

extremely busy R68 road as it makes its way towards Eshowe. The site is easy to find, a signpost directs you off the R68 onto a slip road which passes the battlefield monument and in a couple of hundred yards brings you to the site of the graves of those who were killed in the battle. The cemetery has continued in use over the years and a number of civilian graves have been added. It is believed that the graves were dug close to the west face of the laager. The monument to Lieutenant- Colonel Northey no longer marks his grave as the body was later exhumed by his family and returned to England. To the north can be seen the heights on which the Eshowe mission station was built. A hill, shaped like a small table mountain, forms the highest point of the ridge and is the point from where Pearson's men signalled to the Lower Thukela and also passed on their congratulations to Chelmsford on his victory.

The Gingindlovu battlefield memorial at the turning off the R68 road that leads to the cemetery.

Up at Eshowe the garrison had been able to observe the battle, albeit from a great distance. As soon as the result was clear Pearson flashed his congratulations to Lord Chelmsford. The following day a flying column was organized to proceed to Eshowe and bring out the garrison. The rest of the column remained at Gingindlovu. Despite concerns that the flying column would be attacked again on the final stage of the march nothing materialized. The Zulu army had again suffered heavy casualties and melted away to their homes or places of refuge to recover. By the evening of 3rd April, the seventy-first day of the siege, the garrison of Eshowe was relieved.

The following day the garrison began its return march. For many the joy of rescue was tinged with disappointment over the fact that Chelmsford had decided to abandon the fort after they had worked so hard to construct and defend it. Before he followed Pearson's men, Chelmsford could not resist one last swipe at the Zulu and organized a raid to destroy Dabulamanzi's eZulwini homestead, located just under ten miles away to the west. The march back to the Thukela took four days, long enough for the men to reflect on their comrades who could not make the journey. The siege claimed the lives of twenty-six men,

Relief at last; Chelmsford's column marches into Eshowe along Pearson's new road, 3 April 1879.

left buried in the cemetery at Eshowe, but lying in the wagons of Pearson's slow procession were another 200 men suffering from disease contracted during the siege. Many more of these were to die too, amongst them Captain Warren Wynne, R.E., the architect of Eshowe.

The cemetery at Gingindlovu battlefield. Many of the graves here are civilian ones, post dating the Zulu War.

Chapter Six

SECOND INVASION – DESTRUCTION OF THE ZULU ORDER

The second wave of fighting throughout March and April 1879 had effectively seen the British regain the initiative. King Cetshwayo's armies had been seriously defeated at either end of the country – at Khambula and kwaGingindlovu – within days of one another, and the king had come to realize that a military victory was unlikely. Instead, he tried with increased desperation to open diplomatic channels to discuss peace terms, but in fact both Frere and Lord Chelmsford realized that the war was turning in their favour and neither had anything to gain by compromise. The British aims were once more what they had been in December 1878; the destruction of the king's power by the permanent disbandment of his army.

By this time Chelmsford's forces were being reinforced almost daily, not only by fighting men, but by much-needed General Officers to share his load, by logistical staff and by supplies and material. Throughout April and May Chelmsford re-organized his forces, and prepared to mount a fresh invasion.

Once again, the objective was oNdini (known to the British as Ulundi, a variant spelling of the same word) and once again Chelmsford intended to advance in three separate columns. There were to be no repetitions of the mistakes of January, for this time the columns would be much stronger and would work more closely together. One column, designated the 1st Division, 7,500 strong and made up largely of troops from Pearson's old coastal column and the Eshowe relief column, was to advance up the coast. Chelmsford guessed – rightly, as it turned out – that the Zulu lacked the reserves to make any further defence of the coastal sector and that this column's role would largely be confined to pacification. A new column, composed of reinforcements fresh from home and designated the 2nd Division (5,000 men), was assembled on the border, north of the Centre Column's old start-point at Rorke's Drift. This was to advance by a more northerly route – avoiding the battlefield of Isandlwana, with its melancholy associations – then turn southwards, to join the old Centre Column's projected line of advance. Wood's column (3,200 men), now called the Flying Column, would advance to effect a junction with the 2nd Division and the two would advance in tandem. Together they would provide the main striking arm and be accompanied by Chelmsford himself.

The 1st Division began its advance in the middle of April, establishing two supply depots in Zululand and edging slowly up the coast. The column was plagued by transport problems, but in any case the Zulu did not resist, even when British troops destroyed the royal homesteads of Hlalangubo (know also as 'old oNdini') and emaNgwaneni. Most of the coastal chiefdoms were already exhausted by the war. While many had sent their young men to attend the king's muster at oNdini proper, they no longer had the energy or will to defend their own territories.

The last major action of the war therefore fell to the 2nd Division and Flying Column. The 2nd Division crossed the Ncome river into Zululand on 31st May and almost immediately things went wrong. On the following day, 1 June, the Prince Imperial of France, attached to the British force as an observer, was killed in a skirmish while on reconnaissance. The incident caused a public outcry and had a depressing effect on British morale and was indicative of a new Zulu strategy in central Zululand. While the king had again re-assembled his armies in the hope of mounting one last defence of the heartlands, a greater number of men than usual had remained at their homes and were prepared to harass at each stage of their advance. The change reflected a growing realization that mass attacks in the open were unlikely to succeed, but were proof that the Zulu people's will to resist the invasion had not yet been broken. Just a few days after the Prince Imperial incident, as the columns approached the Ntinini stream, the cavalry screen out in front came under heavy fire from Zulu concealed at the foot of eZungeni mountain and the adjutant of the newly-arrived 17th Lancers was killed.

Chelmsford's reaction was to abandon the pretence that the war was directed solely against King Cetshwayo's administration. Instead, he quite deliberately applied pressure on the Zulu people, hoping to erode their will to resist. His patrols began to destroy civilian homesteads as a matter of course, burning huts, carrying off cattle and despoiling grain-pits. Moreover, the advance was carried out with the same caution which had characterized the Eshowe relief expedition and each night the columns formed laagers around their camps. The British advance was therefore slow and inexorable and it created a trail of devastation in its wake; the king realized that to stop it was as hopeless as warding off a falling tree. Not that the British, even by this stage, were entirely confident of victory. Such was the mystique that had grown up around the Zulu army since Isandlwana that many nights

The British advance during the second invasion of Zululand was characterized by a deliberate attack on Zulu property, in an attempt to exhaust civilian support for the war. Here Irregulars drive looted cattle past a burning homestead.

were disturbed by false alarms, particularly among the inexperienced troops fresh out from England.

Chelmsford's direction joined the planned route of the old Centre Column near Siphezi mountain and followed the spine of the Babanango range towards the Mthonjaneni heights. Here the country fell away spectacularly towards the White Mfolozi and oNdini beyond. To the left of the track, before they descended towards the river, the British passed the head of the emaKhosini valley – the 'place of the kings'– the most sacred spot in Zululand, the original homeland of the Zulu chiefdom and the site of the Royal House's ancestral graves. There were a number of royal homesteads in the valley, venerable establishments which had existed in one form or another since before

The stone redoubt, Fort Nolela, built by the British on the high ground overlooking the White Mfolozi river prior to the battle of oNdini/Ulundi. This was to act as a rallying point if the position was attacked.

King Shaka's time. On 26th June some of Chelmsford's troops descended into the valley and, dispersing detachments of the uNokhenke and uMxhapho regiments who had been posted to guard them, razed them to the ground. This was an act which held terrible omens for the kingdom, for housed at one of them – esiKlebheni – was an artefact of the greatest symbolic importance to the Zulu. Known as the *inkatha yezwe yakwaZulu*, it was a coil of rope which contained items of such mystic importance that they were said to represent the soul of the nation. King Shaka himself had created the coil, which included substances representing all the groups within the kingdom, to the extent that it was widely believed to be the supernatural link which bound the kingdom together. With the burning of the *inkatha*, the nation was poised to fall apart.

The 2nd Division and Flying Column descended from Mthonjaneni on 30th June and the following day established a camp on the southern bank of the White Mfolozi. At last oNdini was within their reach, for Cetshwayo's favourite homestead was just a few miles away on the

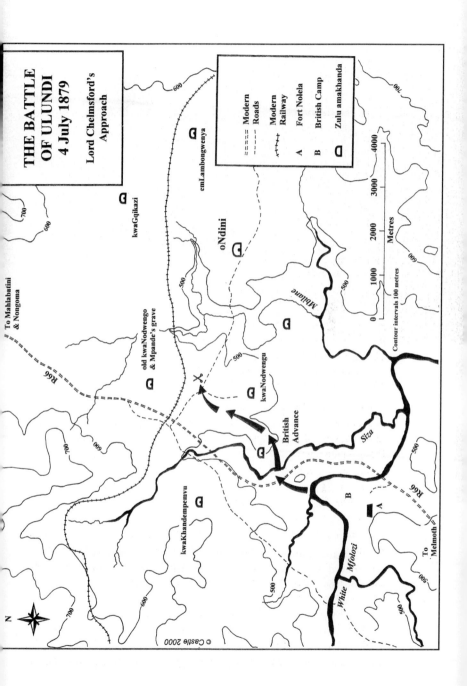

THE BATTLE
OF ULUNDI
4 July 1879

Lord Chelmsford's
Approach

Modern Roads
Modern Railway
A   Fort Nolela
B   British Camp
D   Zulu amakhanda

To Mahlabatini
& Nongoma

R66

kwaGqikazi

emLambongwenya

oNdini

old kwaNodwengo
& Mpande's grave

kwaNodwengu

British Advance

kwaKhandempemvu

Siza

R66

White Mfolozi

To Melmoth

Mbilane

B

A

0   1000   2000   3000   4000
Metres

Contour intervals 100 metres

© Castle 2000

N

British troops relaxing with African auxiliaries on the slopes below Fort Nolela, with the White Mfolozi in the background.

other side, nestling on a plain surrounded by a cluster of similar *amakhanda*. Chelmsford had expected the Zulu to attack as his wagons struggled down from the hills, but in fact the Zulu were saving themselves for one last effort. Indeed, there was one final flurry of diplomatic activity, as Cetshwayo sought to fend off the inevitable. Chelmsford was content to indulge in this charade, as he needed a day or two to make his final preparations, though in fact he was prepared to offer the king no concessions. For two days British troops and Zulu eyed each other warily across the Mfolozi and Zulu snipers, posted among the rocks on bluffs on the northern bank to screen the drifts, took pot-shots at British watering patrols who came down to the river. Yet even the Zulu were growing tired of waiting and, when the king sent a herd of his famous royal white cattle to Chelmsford as a peace offering, his own warriors of the uKhandempemvu regiment refused to let it pass. For all the disasters of the previous months, they were still prepared to fight rather than allow their king to humiliate himself before the invaders.

Hostilities began again on 3rd July. About 500 irregular horseman, commanded by Redvers Buller, crossed the river at drifts above and

120

below the bluffs. Buller's objectives were two-fold; to clear the crossings and to scout the undulating country beyond, to pick out a position from which to fight. The Zulu on the bluffs scattered at their approach and fell back through the long grass towards oNdini. At one point a group of Zulu horsemen appeared on the plain and retired in the same direction. Leaving a reserve to cover his retreat, Buller chased after them. They were only a mile or so from oNdini itself when Buller sensed a trap and called on his men to halt. As they did so, a long line of warriors suddenly rose up from the grass about fifty yards away on their right and fired a ragged volley. Buller had been led into a skilfully prepared ambush; one of the horsemen had been Zibhebhu kaMaphitha himself, the most able and daring of the Zulu commanders and he had been deliberately acting as decoy. Just a few yards ahead of Buller's men, the grass had been carefully plaited to trip the horses, but the trap was sprung prematurely and, fortunately for the British, most of that first Zulu volley was high. As Buller ordered his men to turn about,

A view of the Mahlabathini plain from King Cetshwayo residence at oNdini. The Zulu kings traditionally owned herds of white cattle, and those owned by the present king, H.M. Goodwill Zwelithini, are still kept at oNdini.

The skirmish at oNdini on 3rd July, when Buller's men almost came to grief in a carefully prepared Zulu ambush.

further parties of Zulu rose up on the other side and raced to cut them off. For a mile or two it seemed that they might succeed and Buller lost several men, while others, unhorsed, were snatched up in remarkable acts of heroism from under the Zulus' noses. Only Buller's forethought saved him for, as he raced back towards the river with the Zulu just yards behind him, his reserves came forward in support and their fire caused the Zulu to draw off. Under the circumstances, Buller's casualties were light – three men killed, four wounded and thirteen horses lost.

Nevertheless, Buller had achieved his principle objective and had located the perfect spot from which the British hoped to fight. It was a low rise in the centre of the plain, facing towards oNdini itself. Although the plain was covered in long grass, going brown with the late onset of winter and bush nestled in hollows or along the meandering banks of shallow streams, this position commanded an open view on all sides, with a clear field of fire. Ironically, the Zulu also hoped to fight on the same spot; ever since the success at Isandlwana in January, the young warriors who made up the bulk of the army were convinced that they could overcome the British if only they could catch them in open ground, away from their protective laagers. Both sides, it seems, were keen that the outcome of the final battle should not be in doubt.

Chelmsford crossed the White Mfolozi at dawn on 4th July. He did not take his baggage train with him; his camp on the southern bank of the river would remain the most advanced base established by the British during the war leaving nearly 600 men to guard it. Instead, he took with him just light water and ammunition carts. His force – the largest deployed in battle during the war – consisted of 4,166 white troops, including the 17th Lancers and a detachment of the 1st (King's) Dragoon Guards, 958 black troops, twelve artillery pieces and two Gatling machine-guns. The troops made the crossing unopposed and marched up past the abandoned bluff beyond, towards the oNdini plain. Once they were clear of the river, Chelmsford ordered them to form up in a large rectangle, with the men of Wood's Flying Column along the front face and part of each side and the 2nd Division men completing the box. The NNC and carts were in the centre of the square; the cavalry, both regular and irregular, fanned out on either side to protect the formation while it was on the move, but had been ordered to retire inside when the battle began.

As the sun rose and the early morning mist began to lift, the square

The drift on the White Mfolozi where Lord Chelmsford lead his command across before marching to the battle of oNdini on the Mahlabathini plain. Prior to the battle Zulu marksmen had occupied the bluff on the right and fired on watering parties at the river.

manoeuvred slowly into position, halting several times to allow elements to keep their place. When Chelmsford was entirely satisfied that he was in the best position, he ordered the guns to unlimber and the infantry to take up defensive positions. Five companies of the 80th Regiment held the front face, with two Gatling guns in the centre of their line and two 7 pdrs in the front right corner. The left face consisted of four companies of the 94th Regiment and eight of the 90th, with two 7 pdrs in the centre of the line and two 9 pdrs in the left rear corner. The right face consisted of eight companies of the 1/13th LI and four companies of the 58th, with two 7 pdrs and two 9 pdrs placed along the line and two more 9 pdrs in the right rear corner. The rear face consisted of two companies of the 2/21st and two of the 94th. Several of the infantry battalions had unfurled their Colours and the men were formed up four ranks deep, the front two kneeling, the rear two standing. The square faced towards oNdini, which was about a mile away across the Mbilane stream. Another great royal homestead, kwaNodwengu, was much closer, less than a thousand yards away on the right, while others stood out conspicuously against the surrounding hills.

The first Zulu had come into sight at about 8 am, while the square was still manoeuvring and before the mist had quite burned off. In fact, the king had assembled his army in the week before the battle and most of the regiments who had fought at Isandlwana and Khambula were present in strength. They had been housed in the great *amakhanda*, or were camped in sheltered valleys nearby, while they underwent the necessary rituals to prepare them for combat. Once the British had taken up position, the *amabutho* began to emerge from the homesteads, or out of folds in the ground, or down from the surrounding heights. There were perhaps 25,000 men present altogether and they presented a sinister sight as they drew up in formation, then began to advance, spread out in skirmishing order making good use of whatever cover they could.

Once it was clear that the Zulu did indeed intend to fight, Chelmsford ordered his regular cavalry – for whom such work was considered unsuitable – to retire inside the square, but pushed his irregulars out towards the enemy. As they once had at Khambula, the irregulars rode close to the converging lines of warriors and opened fire at little more than 100 yards' range. This had the desired effect and the Zulu immediately broke into a run. The irregulars fell back towards the square, keeping up a harassing fire and as soon as the nearest Zulu were in range, the artillery opened fire. The infantry moved aside to

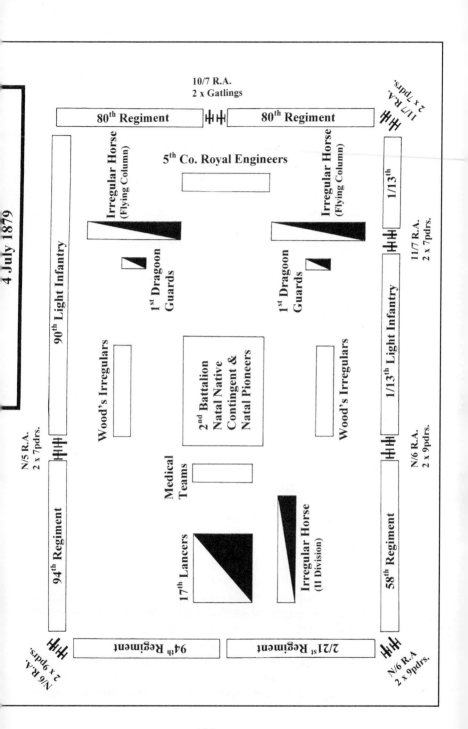

4 July 1879

10/7 R.A.
2 x Gatlings

11/7 R.A.
2 x 7pdrs.

80th Regiment

80th Regiment

Irregular Horse
(Flying Column)

5th Co. Royal Engineers

Irregular Horse
(Flying Column)

1/13th

90th Light Infantry

1st Dragoon Guards

1st Dragoon Guards

11/7 R.A.
2 x 7pdrs.

1/13th Light Infantry

N/5 R.A.
2 x 7pdrs.

Wood's Irregulars

2nd Battalion Natal Native Contingent & Natal Pioneers

Wood's Irregulars

94th Regiment

Medical Teams

17th Lancers

Irregular Horse
(II Division)

58th Regiment

N/6 R.A.
2 x 9pdrs.

N/6 R.A.
2 x 9pdrs.

94th Regiment

2/21st Regiment

N/6 R.A
2 x 9pdrs.

allow the irregulars to enter and the battle began in earnest.

Some of those present inside the square, who had seen the Zulu attack at Khambula, were later to claim that the Zulu attacks at oNdini were half-hearted. Certainly, the cumulative blows of the last six months had destroyed much of the belligerent confidence of January and indeed many of the bravest and most resourceful *izinduna* had already been killed. But if the Zulu did not persist in their attacks as they once had at Khambula, some of their initial assaults were scarcely less determined. Completely encircling the square on all sides, they advanced unevenly, until the infantry opened fire at about 200 yards' range. Expecting to find the British rear unprotected, as they had at Isandlwana, the Zulu were taken aback to find it secure on all sides. Mangwanana Mchunu of the uVe regiment recalled their confusion:

'Men of every regiment I spoke to after, who had attacked on
other sides to where we attacked, said that the soldiers were
facing them. We said the soldiers were facing us and yet others
at the side of us said they were facing them ...'

The infantry fired volleys by sections and a terrible noise, like a great rip of thunder, rippled round the square. Soon all four faces were wreathed in smoke and several times Chelmsford ordered a cease-fire, to allow the smoke to clear. Certainly the smoke rendered such fire less effective than it might otherwise have been, for the Zulu could be seen only as fleeting targets, bobbing through the long grass. Nevertheless, the psychological effect to those on the receiving end was awesome and survivors later recalled the almost physical shock of the noise and concussion. According to Sofikasho Zungu, a warrior of the iNgobamakhosi,

'...there was one great roar from the big guns. I could see
flames from the guns and smoke from them and also the flames
of the [rockets] that I saw at Khambula ... there was such a roar
of guns that we were utterly bewildered. One shot went close to
my head and I fell down and thought I was dead. I saw one [Zulu]
whose head was struck off right next to me and his body stood
up shivering with hands clenched until it fell ...'

Here and there groups of warriors rose out of the grass to make a desperate rush, only to be scythed down wholesale before they could reach within twenty yards of the British position. On the front face the Gatling guns chopped clear paths through the advancing lines but were not enough to prevent one determined *induna* from leading a charge straight at them; he was shot down just as he reached the carriages. Generally, the guns were brutally effective when they worked, but

Another view of the Mahlabathini from oNdini. The white speck, directly below the flat topped hill, is the dome of the battlefield memorial. Hedges, which roughly mark the position of the British square, form the dark area around the dome.

several times they broke down during the action; the bolts had a tendency to slip out and were difficult to find in the long grass, while as soon as the guns became hot the thin brass cartridges tore, fouling the breaches.

The most determined attack was on the right rear corner. Here a column of young warriors – apparently the iNgobamakhosi and uVe *amabutho* and led by Zibhebhu kaMaphitha – had advanced close to the British position under cover of the kwaNodwengu homestead. The British had deliberately set the complex on fire and now the Zulu made use of the thick, billowing smoke. Gathering just out of sight of the British line, they suddenly made a fierce dash on the corner. Chelmsford, who with his staff had been riding round inside the square directing the defence, rode over and ordered a company of Royal Engineers, who had been in reserve, forward to support the line. Melton Prior, the war artist, who had been sketching the battle,

'... ran down to where the 21st and 58th Regiments were heavily engaged with some Zulu, said to be 6,000 strong and 30 deep, who were charging and it was then that I heard Lord Chelmsford say to the troops, "Men, fire faster; can't you fire faster" ... the terrific fire from our men made them stagger, halt

A dramatic picture which suggests something of the formidable array of British firepower deployed at Ulundi. Rai England Collection

and fall back in a straggling mass, leaving a heap of dead and dying on the ground.

'I have read since various statements as to how near the enemy got to our square and it is often stated that twenty to thirty paces is the closest, but I can say that I personally went out and reached the nearest one in nine paces, so their onslaught was pretty determined.'

Once the first rushes subsided, the Zulu settled down in the long grass and opened a heavy fire on the square. In theory such a formation should have been acutely vulnerable to rifle fire, but the presence of several hundred Martini-Henry rifles captured at Isandlwana was not sufficient to over-ride the poor quality of most Zulu firearms and marksmanship. Although most of Chelmsford's casualties were caused by firearms, most of the Zulu bullets went high and the air above the square hummed and hissed with hot metal, to the occasional discomfort of mounted men.

The last main assault was attempted from oNdini itself. A column of several thousand warriors, mostly older men associated with the homestead itself, formed up in the central enclosure and advanced down the slope towards the square. As they emerged from the complex, however, the artillery on the front face began to drop shells skilfully among them forcing the column to halt and retire.

It was now about 9.15 – little more than an hour from the first Zulu appearance – and the attacks were clearly flagging. Over the next fifteen minutes, some elements could clearly be seen withdrawing and at about 9.30 Chelmsford judged the moment right for a decisive blow. The infantry on the rear face were ordered to move aside and the 17th Lancers were ordered out of the square. To their colonel, Drury Curzon Drury-Lowe, Chelmsford called out cheerily 'Go at them Lowe!' The 17th formed into line for a charge, sweeping in gathering momentum across the grassland towards the distant hills. Although the lance was already largely obsolete in conventional European warfare, it was ideal in circumstances such as these and the heavy English chargers

Inside the square at the height of the battle; a noisy and confusing mass of animals and men waiting to go into action. Lord Chelmsford, centre.

Perhaps one of the most accurate representations of the British position; the infantry on the right have marched aside to let the 17th Lancers emerge.

scattered the Zulu in front of them, the riders skewering them as they ran. Behind the 17th came the irregular cavalry, who followed in their wake, shooting down any warriors who had managed to escape the lance. George Mossop, a young trooper in the Frontier Light Horse, found a horrible fascination in the almost Medieval mechanics of such killing:

'On their great imported horses they sat bolt upright, their long lances held perfectly erect, the lance heads glittering in the sunshine.

'They formed into line. In one movement the lances dropped to the right side of the horses' necks, a long level line of poles, stretching out a distance in front of the horses, the steel heads pointing straight at the mass of retreating Zulu. As the big horses bounded forward and thundered into them, each lance point pierced the Zulu in front of it; the man fell and as the horse

130

passed on beyond him the lance was withdrawn, lifted and thrust forward into another Zulu in front.

'The movement of withdrawing the lance and again getting it into position was very rapid; I could not quite understand how it was done. It was such a mix for us riding behind the Lancers, with our horses jumping over dead Zulu and having to deal with those who were knocked down by the Lancer horses but not pierced, that we did not have the opportunity to study the work...'

In a very short time, the Zulu retreat collapsed into rout. Only when the Lancers reached the foot of the hills did the Zulu attempt a stand, a body of young warriors suddenly standing up in the long grass and firing a volley, which killed Captain Wyatt-Edgell of the 17th. The charge began to lose momentum on the slope and a straggling close-quarter fight broke out, until the 17th retired to regroup. It then fell to the artillery to take up the challenge, raining shells on any Zulu concentration that showed signs of lingering.

Indeed, the British pursuit after the battle was particularly ruthless. In the elation of victory, most of those on the British side were only too glad to have an opportunity to avenge Isandlwana and any Zulu lying wounded or sheltering near the square had little hope of mercy. While

An incident during the battle; a Lancer is unhorsed and surprised by two warriors, while a companion gallops to his rescue.

Keen to inflict a decisive blow, the British showed no mercy to exhausted warriors during the pursuit.

the cavalry flushed out groups on the far edges of the plain, the NNC were sent out to scour the area immediately around the square and they thoroughly and efficiently despatched any living warriors they found. For the survivors of the battle it was clear the war was over. One Zulu who was taken prisoner expressed the view of many,

'We had no idea the white force was so strong in numbers till we saw it in the open... and we were startled by the number of horsemen... we were completely beaten off by the artillery and bullets... The army is now thoroughly beaten and as we were beaten in the open, it will not reassemble or fight again.'

The battle was over by about 9.45 am. Chelmsford had lost two officers and ten men killed, one officer mortally wounded and sixty-nine men injured. The dead were buried in the centre of the square and, once the wounded had been made comfortable, Chelmsford ordered the square to advance towards oNdini. It halted on the banks of the Mbilane where the men were allowed to fill their water bottles. Already, the cavalry were riding around the plain and setting fire to the

After the charge; the 17th Lancers re assemble.

An historic photograph: the only one taken during the war which actually shows an incident in progress. Smoke from oNdini (right) and the battlefield (left), photographed from the camp at Fort Nolela.

The battlefield of oNdini. This view is from the rear face of the square, looking westwards. Two companies of the 2/21st Regiment and two of the 94th Regiment manned this face of the square.

great *amakhanda* and Chelmsford allowed some of his officers to ride forward to oNdini. There was a rush for the king's personal quarters at the far end, for tales of Zulu treasure had circulated among the British troops, but in fact it was found to be deserted, with nothing of intrinsic value. Nevertheless, the officers collected up what souvenirs they could and then began to set fire to the huts.

Anyone visiting the modern town of Ulundi today can approach by major highway, either from Lord Chelmsford's direction of advance – from Dundee via Babanango – or from the coastal sector, via Melmoth. The main approach road descends from the Mthonjaneni heights along roughly the same route used by Chelmsford and the last British campsite in Zululand is signposted 'Fort Nolela' to the left of the road,

The destruction of oNdini. Chelmsford advances his square to the banks of the Mbilane stream, to witness the burning of the royal homestead.

just before the White Mfolozi bridge. Modern Ulundi consists of several separate blocks, scattered across the plain, with traditional dwellings in between. A large stone monument, topped with a silver dome, lies near the small airfield and marks the site of Chelmsford's square.

It is surrounded by a thorn hedge which, while it is neither exactly aligned, nor quite the right size, does give an impression of the approximate area enclosed within the square. It is usually quiet and peaceful within the enclosure, a far cry from the noisy chaos of battle, the crowd of animals and men, the chattering Gatlings, booming guns, crashing volleys, the constant whine of bullets passing overhead and the shouts of 'uSuthu!' and cries of pain from beyond the lines. There are plaques on the walls of the monument commemorating the dead, including one to 'the brave warriors who fell here in defence of the old Zulu order', which until recently was the only memorial erected to the Zulu dead.

The British casualties are buried beyond the memorial and it is from this position that one gets the best impression of the battlefield. The dark curve of the partially reconstructed homestead of oNdini – the alternative spelling is used to distinguish it from modern Ulundi – is visible on the slope ahead, while kwaNodwengu was on the falling ground to the right. Other amakhanda were situated on the hills to the left of oNdini and at the foot of the distinctive twin peaks directly to the rear.

From the monument it is an easy drive up the slope to oNdini. Here archaeologists have reconstructed part of the king's enclosure over the original remains of the hut floors. Although only a small proportion of the entire homestead has been rebuilt, it is enough to give an idea of its former splendour in the days when it consisted of nearly 1,500 huts and was alive with thousands of people and cattle. The small museum nearby includes some fascinating displays of the Zulu way of life.

Chelmsford began his withdrawal early in the afternoon. Lines of cartridge cases in the grass marked the site of the square and in a great circle around it lay the Zulu dead, whom the British made no effort to bury. Estimates of their number vary, but most sources agree on a figure of about 1,500. Over the next few days, some were identified and buried by friends and relatives, but many were left where they fell. The royal homesteads continued to burn for four days after the battle, while the field was littered with human bones for decades to come.

For Chelmsford, the war was over and he immediately began to

The British graves at oNdini. These casualties were buried within the confines of the square before the men marched off.

withdraw his troops. He had avenged the disaster at Isandlwana and the victory had taken the sting out of the news that he was to be replaced. His successor, Sir Garnet Wolseley, was already in the country and Chelmsford was content to hand over his command and return to England. He was showered with honours and titles by a grateful establishment but he never commanded an army in the field again.

It was left to Wolseley to suppress what pockets of resistance remained and to implement a peace settlement. He reorganized Chelmsford's troops and sent columns to pacify the outlying districts. It was not until September that the last shots were fired in skirmishes in the north of the country. In the aftermath of oNdini, however, most Zulu were exhausted by the war and returned quietly to their homes. While most remained loyal to the person of the king, they realized that his power was finished. Cetshwayo had not waited to see the final humiliation of his army but had retired into the hills with his household. He was captured by British Dragoons in the remote Ngome forest at the end of August.

Wolseley had already disposed of his kingdom. Britain had turned its back on the policy of Confederation which had led to the war and Wolseley's brief was to reduce the power of the kingdom to threaten its colonial neighbours, without unnecessary political entanglement. His solution was to divide the country up among thirteen chiefs, who were perceived to share British interests and to be hostile to the Zulu Royal House.

It was a classic case of 'divide and rule' and it brought untold misery to the Zulu people. Many of the chiefs were regarded as traitors by their own people and the country soon split along pro- and anti-royalist lines. Within three years, Zululand would collapse into a brutal and bloody civil war, which cost more lives than had the British invasion and which would see the final destruction of Shaka's kingdom.

IN MEMORY OF

THE BRAVE WARRIORS WHO FELL

HERE IN 1879 IN DEFENCE OF THE

OLD ZULU ORDER

_____

The simple marble tablet, located within the battlefield monument, which commemorates the sacrifice of the Zulu warriors who died at oNdini, 4th July 1879, the last battle of the Anglo-Zulu War.

Further Reading

The literature on the Anglo-Zulu War is immense. The following titles are recommended by the authors for their particular relevance to the battles covered in this book.

Emery, Frank, *The Red Soldier; Letters from the Zulu War*, London 1979.

Castle, Ian, and Knight, Ian, *Fearful Hard Times; The Siege and Relief of Eshowe*, London, 1994.

Drooglever, R.W.F., *The Road to Isandhlwana*; Colonel Anthony Durnford in Natal and Zululand, London, 1992.

Laband, John, and Thompson, Paul, *The Illustrated Guide to the Anglo-Zulu War,* Pietermaritzburg, 2000.

Laband, John, *Rope of Sand* (published in the UK under the title *The Rise and Fall of the Zulu Kingdom*), Johannesburg, 1995.

Laband, John, *The Battle of Ulundi*, Pietermaritzburg and Ulundi, 1988.

Laband, John, and Knight, Ian, *The War Correspondents; The Anglo-Zulu War*, London, 1998.

Laband, John, and Mathews, Jeff, *Isandlwana*, Pietermaritzburg and Ulundi 1992.

Knight, Ian, and Castle, Ian, *The Zulu War; Then and Now*, London, 1993.

Knight, Ian, *Zulu; The Battles of Isandlwana and Rorke's Drift*, London, 1992.

Knight, Ian, *The Anatomy of the Zulu Army*, London, 1993.

Knight, Ian, *Great Zulu Battles*, London, 1997.

Knight, Ian, *Great Zulu Commanders*, London, 1998.

INDEX

144